MEATY BEATY BIG AND BOUNCY
ORIGINAL SOUNDTRACK OF THE PARAMOUNT MOTION PICTURE
Songs In The Key
Stevie
COLUMBIA
Kind of Blue
with Julian "Cannonball" Adderley
Paul Chambers
James Cobb
John Coltrane
Bill Evans
Wynton Kelly
RECORDED LIVE AT THE FAMOUS APOLLO THEATRE, NEW YORK CITY
DAVID BOWIE
ZIGGY STARDUST

BOOZE AND VINYL

A SPIRITED GUIDE TO
GREAT MUSIC & MIXED DRINKS

ANDRÉ DARLINGTON & TENAYA DARLINGTON

PHOTOGRAPHY BY JASON VARNEY

RUNNING PRESS
PHILADELPHIA

Running Press
Hachette Book Group
1290 Avenue of the Americas, New York, NY 10104
www.runningpress.com
@Running_Press

Printed in China

First Edition: May 2018

Published by Running Press, an imprint of Perseus Books, LLC, a subsidiary of Hachette Book Group, Inc.
The Running Press name and logo is a trademark of the Hachette Book Group

The Hachette Speakers Bureau provides a wide range of authors for speaking events.
To find out more, go to www.hachettespeakersbureau.com or call (866) 376-6591.

The publisher is not responsible for websites (or their content) that are not owned by the publisher.

Print book cover and interior design by Joshua McDonnell.

Library of Congress Control Number: 2017954158

ISBNs: 978-0-7624-6347-3 (hardcover), 978-0-7624-6348-0 (ebook),
978-0-7624-9322-7 (ebook), 978-0-7624-9323-4 (ebook)

1010

10 9

Additional Photography:
© Getty Images: gerisima p. 42; itskatjas p. 44–45; Freder p. 68; surashetkhamsuk p. 69; FGorgun p. 74; haushe p. 74; Twoellis p. 76; chipstudio p. 96; Ekaterina Romanova p. 96–97; DanHenson1 p. 111; donfiore p. 124; halbergman p. 126; lucky-photographer p. 128–130;sestevens p. 142; borchee p. 143 and 145; THEPALMER p. 147; Nikada p. 148; tareo81 p. 165; supermimicry p. 174; Miroslav_1 p. 185

© Joshua McDonnell pp. 62, 65, 70–71, 84–85, 87–88, 92–93, p114–115, 132–133, 152, 154, 162, 179–181, 188, 200–203

TO MUSIC LOVERS EVERYWHERE:

ESPECIALLY JEFF STREGIEL AND CHARMAINE CASTLE; WHO INSPIRED US TO STRUM THE FIRST CHORDS OF THIS PROJECT.

MUSIC IS
THAT FILLS THE

THE WINE
CUP OF SILENCE.

—ROBERT FRIPP

CONTENTS

THE SOUND O

We grew up flipping records on our dad's Thorens turntable and have spent most of our adult lives hosting parties together and following the drinks beat as food journalists. After writing a craft cocktail bible (*The New Cocktail Hour*) and pairing cocktails with classic film (in *Turner Classic Movies: Movie Night Menus*), the two of us felt inspired to

a car on a dark highway. We loved succumbing to the feeling of being enveloped by music. Today, we return to those moments again and again. Can you imagine a time when friends went to one another's houses to listen to LPs together? It's returned.

The renaissance of the long-playing record has brought back the listening session: playing

return to something formative: the listening party.

Our family record player held center stage in the living room, and some of our favorite memories are of our parents' vinyl parties. Picture candles flickering, adults sacked out with Gin and Tonics. In the semidarkness, the amp and tuner of our father's hi-fi glowed like the dashboard of

one album, all the way through—preferably with a drink in hand. Between the appealing sound of vinyl and the sense of nostalgia they elicit, LPs possess an enduring quality that we crave. The album art. The poetic hisses and pops. These are the elements of a rich and deeply personal musical experience, without earbuds. And whether you've

F SUBSTANCE

just bought your first LP or have spent your life digging through record bins, the musical selections in these pages offer a taste of some of the most appealing albums ever recorded.

This book is for anyone with an itch to explore timeless music and mixed drinks together. Whether you're a beer and shot drinker or some-

some of the best wax ever pressed in order to achieve a whole new level of listening enjoyment. Don't know how to serve a proper Martini? We'll show you how. With a few tips and techniques in the back of this book, you'll be a mix-master before the first record is over.

LPs have carved out a place in our psyche—

ECORD, YOU DON'T REALLY OWN THE ALBUM. —JACK WHITE, THE WHITE STRIPES

one with a cabinet full of coupes, the recipes you'll find in these pages are designed to enhance your musical experience. We've got simple solutions (loads of two- and three-ingredient recipes), a wide range of classic cocktails, and we also discovered some lesser-known gems. So get ready to shake and stir—and just plain pour—your way through

maybe due to nostalgia, a love of the sound quality, or the desire for a tangible medium in the digital age. We think it's also because they offer an experience that cannot be duplicated any other way. And we are thrilled to invite you to join us in the once-again flourishing activity of combining booze and vinyl.

How This Book Is Organized

In these pages, you'll find seventy groundbreaking albums from the 1930s through the 2000s. We've organized them into four chapters, depending on the mood—Rock, Dance, Chill, and Seduce. Within each chapter, the albums are arranged chronologically.

Every album includes a Side A and Side B cocktail to round out a two-drink listening session. For each entry, you'll also find liner notes about the artist and album, along with a party idea ("When to Spin") if you feel like embracing the album's vibe with a chill-out grill-out (page 160) or a full-on dance party complete with a catwalk (page 91). Small plate recipes? We've got a few of those, too, if you need some munchies.

Keep in mind that the best listening parties are fun and fluid, so don't be afraid to mix and match.

HOW TO HOST A BOOZY LISTENING PARTY

Our Bar Code chapter (page 206) has all the tips and techniques you need to make great drinks, including instructions on shaking, stirring, and more. If you're planning a party, just remember: advance prep is key. You don't want to miss out on a listening adventure because you're running down the street to get ice. Here's a checklist:

- Glassware in the freezer, chilling

- Fresh ice, so that it doesn't taste stale

- Tools out, if needed (shaker, cocktail glass, jigger, etc.—see our list of bar merch, page 214)

- Fresh citrus, cut and juiced (up to a few hours in advance)

- The albums you're going to play, out and in order

The recent resurgence of craft cocktails has brought a bit more technical know-how to the table. But it's all meant to ensure one thing: better drinks! A few details to note:

- Recipes for simple syrup and homemade grenadine are in the back (page 212).

- Demerara sugar is our choice for cocktails— we like the rich taste and the fact that it is less processed. Feel free to use plain white granulated sugar.

- When we say "cocktail glass," we mean a martini or coupe glass (the drink is served "up"—i.e., without ice).

- When we say a "dash" we technically mean just a drop, about ⅛ of a teaspoon.

- Liquor brands are included only when they are specified by the original recipe creator.

- When a drink calls for Maraschino (cherry) liqueur, we get the best results with Luxardo.

- Batching instructions for cocktails are on page 216.

OUR FAVORITE
TWO- AND THREE-INGREDIENT DRINKS

If simplicity is your goal, here are more than fifty easy sippers,
which are great listening session go-tos.

Two-Ingredient

Three-Ingredient

CHAPTER 1

ROCK

The albums in this chapter are total ragers. When you want to feel the euphoria of rock's greatest moments or let out a little aggression, these records unleash the restless animal within.

From the Ramones' punk antics to Beck's space cowboy jukebox, you've got LPs that will start parties and burn the house down. Our drink pairings include a classic Dirty Martini (page 33), simple shots like the Kamikaze (page 45), and even a full-on Whiskey Tasting (page 52).

Want to skip the polite drinks? Keep it simple with an easy beer and a chaser. 'Cuz who wants to spend time shaking drinks in the kitchen during "Born to Run"? Want to set up a rockin' drink station? Take a look at our AC/DC wet bar (page 41). And if you want some great nosh, drop the needle on Led Zeppelin *IV* (page 21), fire up the grill, and jump into our recipe for a Led Zep-loin!

Rolling Stones

Led Zeppelin

Bruce Springsteen

Queen

The Ramones

Iggy Pop

The Cars

The Clash

Joy Division

AC/DC

Beastie Boys

Guns N' Roses

Beck

The White Stripes

STICKY FINGERS
ROLLING STONES

1971 // GENRE: **ROCK 'N' ROLL, BLUES** // WHEN TO SPIN: **BOOZY BRUNCH**

LINER NOTES

This record is dirty. From Andy Warhol's album cover of a blue jeans–clad crotch to the louche lyrics, *Sticky Fingers* is all bravado and sleaze. Prepare to rock, sway, testify, and boogie to the Stones' ninth studio album and the first one without former leader Brian Jones. This is also the first time the band's signature lips logo appears. It's based on the Hindu goddess Kali. Welcome to peak Stones—giddyup on those wild horses!

BEFORE YOU DROP THE NEEDLE

Roll into breakfast with "Brown Sugar" by glazing some cinnamon rolls or voting somebody to make pancakes. *Sticky Fingers* is our go-to New Year's Day brunch album.

A

TEQUILA SUNRISE

In his epic autobiography, *Life*, Keith Richards calls the Stones' legendary cross-country tour in 1972 the "Cocaine and Tequila Sunrise" tour. Legend has it, a bartender in Sausalito offered lead singer Mick Jagger his first taste of the drink, and it became a favorite.

1½ ounces tequila

3 ounces fresh orange juice

½ ounce grenadine (recipe, page 212)

Orange slice, for garnish

Add tequila and orange juice to a rocks glass filled with ice. Then add grenadine. Do not stir. The grenadine will naturally sink to the bottom. Garnish with an orange slice.

B

JACK AND COKE (AND COORS)

The Stones spent time recording at the famed Muscle Shoals Sound Studio on the Tennessee River, which is maybe where Keith picked up his Jack Daniel's habit. In many pictures from this era, he's got a bottle with him, along with Coke and Coors. Time to get sloppy and start the record all over again.

2 ounces Jack Daniel's whiskey

1 can (12-ounce) Coca-Cola

1 can (12-ounce) Coors

Line up whiskey, Coke, and Coors and sip from all three in turn until finished.

Producer: Jimmy Miller   Label: Atlantic

IV

LED ZEPPELIN

1971 // GENRE: **HARD ROCK, BLUES ROCK, FOLK ROCK**
WHEN TO SPIN: **RITUAL SACRIFICE (I.E., BARBECUE MEAT PARTY)**

LINER NOTES ||| Like a group of howling druids summoning the rock gods, Zeppelin's *IV* is bombastic and BIG. Interestingly, it was recorded in a Victorian mansion where the band took breaks to roam the grounds with cups of tea in hand. The fourth Zeppelin album was the result of perseverance and confidence. While it is officially untitled, the *IV* stands for the four members of the band. The album included an eight-minute song, which at the time was considered commercial suicide. That song is "Stairway to Heaven." The album crushed sales records. Get ready to drink and party along to the band's most beloved songs.

BEFORE YOU DROP THE NEEDLE ||| Prep a Led Zep-loin (oh, yes we did!) see page 24

Producer: Roy Thomas Baker   Label: EMI

HELLFIRE PUNCH

Jam band elements, such as lengthy improvised passages, pervade the album, diverging from the short, discreet "song-based" format of Zeppelin's contemporaries. For this reason, we honor these free-range rockers with a communal punch bowl, rather than individual drinks. Guitarist Jimmy Page, as you might know, was into some seriously weird shit (think: devil worship) at the time—so we're pleased to offer this punch, the pride and joy of Britain's most mischievous and satanic eighteenth-century men's club, the Hellfire Club. Unearthed by cocktail historian David Wondrich, this recipe is sure to fire up an obsession with the occultist Aleister Crowley.

SERVES 20 TO 30

3 bottles (750 ml) brandy (preferably Ferrand 1840 Cognac)

1 bottle (750 ml) rum (preferably Smith & Cross Jamaican Rum)

1 bottle (750ml) cherry brandy (preferably Luxardo Sangue Morlacco)

16 lemons, zested

2 pounds demerara sugar

1 gallon warm water

17 ounces (a little over 2 cups) fresh lemon juice

2 nutmegs, grated

1 tablespoon ground cayenne pepper

8 cups milk, heated to a simmer

Steep lemon zest in brandy, rum, and cherry brandy overnight. Dissolve the demerara sugar in warm water, then let it cool and add it to the spirits mixture. Add lemon juice, nutmeg, cayenne, and milk. Yes, the milk will curdle.

Allow the punch to sit for 1 hour, then strain it through a cheesecloth. Strain again, pouring the liquid over the retained curds.

Serve in a large punch bowl with a big block of ice.

LED ZEP-LOIN

Inspired by the British heritage of these rockers, we felt called to add hard cider to our favorite Sunday pork roast recipe. It smells divine while cooking and makes everyone happy when you pull it out of the oven. Don't forget to set a timer and add the apples during the last 45 minutes of cooking. We like to serve this loin with boiled new potatoes smothered in butter and topped with chopped parsley. If you prefer to grill the loin, just prepare the apple mixture on the stovetop.

1 (4-pound) boneless pork loin,

   with fat still intact

2 tablespoons olive oil

2 teaspoons sea salt

¾ cup hard cider

¾ cup chicken stock

4 shallots, peeled

2 cloves garlic, crushed

3 large red apples, such as Pink Lady

Preheat the oven to 475°F. Pat the loin dry, then score the surface with parallel slits ¼ inch to ½ inch apart. Rub the loin with olive oil and then salt. Roast for 30 minutes.

Reduce temperature to 325°F, add cider, stock, shallots, and garlic. Roast for another 2 to 2½ hours, or until the inner temperature reaches 145°F. During the last 45 minutes, add the apples.

Remove the roast and let it rest for 20 minutes before carving. Serve on a platter with the apples and juices surrounding it.

BORN TO RUN
BRUCE SPRINGSTEEN

1975
Genre: Rock 'n' Roll
When to Spin: Friday after work

LINER NOTES

Brimming with ambition, Springsteen's third studio album brought him mainstream success. The stakes were high because the "Boss" had already been hailed as the future of rock 'n' roll. He had a big budget. Everything was riding on this make-or-break release. The pressure (Springsteen spent six months honing the song "Born to Run" alone) produced a glorious masterpiece of Americana. It's an ode to classic rock themes, including the romanticism of the open road. Imagine the convertible top down with the wind in your face, and you've got the exuberant feel of this vinyl essential.

BEFORE YOU DROP THE NEEDLE

Slip into your cutoffs, prop the back door open, and fire up the grill. Then, sit on your porch and chill. Or, hey, why not crank the music and wax your hubcaps?

SIDE A
BOILERMAKER

Pull out a six-pack and a bottle of bourbon. Keep it simple.

1 can inexpensive beer

1 shot bourbon

Serve side by side.

SIDE B
NEW JERSEY COCKTAIL

Verdant New Jersey was known during colonial times for its apple orchards and its cider production. The original Jersey Cocktail calls for hard cider. Take it up a notch with applejack. Think of this as an apple-y Old Fashioned. Perfect for this Jersey boy.

2 ounces applejack

2 dashes Angostura bitters

1 teaspoon granulated sugar

Stir ingredients with ice and strain into a chilled cocktail glass.

Producers: Bruce Springsteen, Mike Appel, Jon Landau   Label: Columbia

QUEEN

A NIGHT AT THE OPERA

LINER NOTES Queen's fourth studio album appeared over the holidays in November of '75. And, trust us, it totally works as a holiday album—if a very grandiose and glam one. The most expensive record ever made at the time, it stirred together a crazy blend of hard rock antics and classical influences. Plus, lots of a cappella. The album roared to the top of the charts with the extravagant hit "Bohemian Rhapsody" enduring as one of the greatest songs of all time. The song was famously relaunched to popularity by the 1992 movie *Wayne's World*. **BEFORE YOU DROP THE NEEDLE** Invite your guests to wear their most heinous sweaters and bring casseroles.

Genre:
Rock, Pop, Hard Rock, Glam Rock

When to Spin:
Holiday headbanger

SIDE A
Coronation Cocktail

Obvi, it's Queen—the night must begin with a Coronation! This regal cocktail is an ideal aperitif with holiday nibbles. Don't forget to toast the late rock legend Freddie Mercury, whose voice here is a kind of anointment.

1½ ounces amontillado sherry
1½ ounces dry vermouth
¼ ounce Maraschino liqueur
2 dashes orange bitters
Lemon twist, for garnish

Stir ingredients with ice and strain into a chilled cocktail glass. Garnish with a lemon twist.

SIDE B
Bohemian Cocktail

Is this the real life or just fantasy? This tasty quaffer, featuring elderflower liqueur in balance with tart grapefruit, is easy come, easy go.

1½ ounces London dry gin
1 ounce St-Germain liqueur
2 dashes Peychaud's bitters
1 ounce fresh pink grapefruit juice

Shake ingredients with ice and strain into a chilled cocktail glass.

Bonus Track Check out the Marx Brothers' *A Night at the Opera*, the film that inspired this album's title. The band saw it one night at the studio. Also, be sure to queue up the video of Queen at Live Aid 1985, one of the greatest live performances of all time.

RAMO

THE RAMONES
1976
GENRE: **PUNK ROCK** WHEN TO SPIN: **GARAGE PARTY**

Liner notes: By the late '70s, mainstream radio featured long guitar solos noodling to nowhere. The Ramones responded by calling bullshit and returning to rock's rebellious roots with sharp, up-tempo songs only a couple of minutes long. Wearing the rockabilly and greaser outfit of jeans, white T-shirts, and motorcycle jackets, this band from Queens leaped onto the scene and shaped the aesthetic of modern rock 'n' roll. In the swirl of '80s economic woes, punk's nihilism and anti-establishment swagger attracted fans by the droves. The debut of this LP was huge, influencing bands like the Sex Pistols, the Buzzcocks, and the Clash, and kicking off a full-blown punk scene on both sides of the pond.

ONES

Before you drop the needle: Turn your garage into a clubhouse. Cover the windows with black paper, set up a DIY wet bar (a plywood door clamped to some sawhorses works fine), and string up some twinkly lights.

A

WHISKEY SMASH

An old drink with a punk rock name! This nineteenth-century cooler is boozy yet still mighty refreshing. Originally prepared with "fruits in season," it can be made year-round with lemons. Think of it as a Mint Julep with a citrus edge.

2 ounces bourbon

½ ounce simple syrup (page 213)

Half a lemon, cut into four pieces

4 mint leaves, plus a few sprigs for garnish

Crushed ice

Muddle the mint leaves with simple syrup and lemon in a cocktail glass or shaker. Add bourbon and pour the mixture into a rocks glass. Fill the glass with crushed ice and garnish with mint.

B

JELL-O SHOTS

Jiggly and boozy, adult Jell-O shots will always be a favorite and they're mobile (no sloshing)! Pick any flavor you wish, and freeze in ice cube trays of any shape. Oh, snap! It's like you're twenty-one again.

1½ cups vodka

1 box (3-ounce) Jell-O

Combine vodka with ½ cup of ice-cold water in a bowl. In a pitcher or large measuring cup, whisk Jell-O into 1 cup of boiling water. Stir in the chilled alcohol mixture. Pour into paper cups or into ice trays (lightly grease them for easy removal). Pop the shots into the fridge for 2 to 4 hours, or until set.

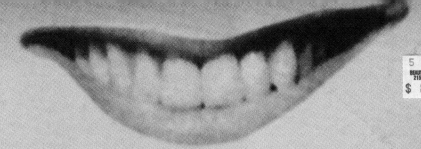

IGGY POP

LUST FOR LIFE

1977   Genre: Rock, Garage Rock, Punk Rock   When to Spin: Pregaming before a show

LINER NOTES

Hold the beating heart of the night in your hand. If his previous David Bowie collaboration, *The Idiot*, was a reticent album that prefigured goth and industrial, Iggy Pop's second solo effort channeled pure hand-clapping, sing-along rock 'n' roll. Recorded in Berlin while both he and Bowie were struggling with addiction, Pop unleashes all the exuberance of a fresh will to live. *Lust* explodes with raw energy, and it's evident that the artistic competition with Bowie pushed Pop's writing to new heights—from the immortal title song "Lust for Life" to "The Passenger." If there's one Iggy album to raise a glass to, this is it. And if it's not a Martini or a Corpse Reviver, make it a glass of white wine—just like in the song "Fall in Love with Me."

BEFORE YOU DROP THE NEEDLE

This is *the* album to listen to while you're prepping for a night out with friends.

A DIRTY MARTINI

The ultimate three-ingredient cocktail, a Dirty Martini may be the lustiest way to begin an evening. It's certainly a rockin' classic with many variations, since every type of gin and vermouth yield a different taste. If you're new to the Martini game, try a London dry–style gin—we love its bracing juniper flavor. And always be sure your vermouth is fresh (note: store it in the fridge after opening the bottle). Finally, using decent olives makes all the difference. Our go-tos are plump, bright green Castelvetrano olives, which you can find at olive bars or in jars at the grocery.

2½ ounces gin

½ ounce dry vermouth

½ ounce olive brine, to taste

Olive, for garnish

Stir ingredients with ice and strain into a chilled cocktail glass. Garnish with an olive.

B CORPSE REVIVER (No. 2)

Corpse Revivers are a classification of breakfast cocktails designed to wake the dead—or just the very hungover. The No. 2 became popular when it was included in *The Savoy Cocktail Book* in 1930. This drink remains a bar staple and provides a perfect dose of energy, as well as a spectral touch of absinthe. Note: Cocchi Americano is a delicious Italian aperitif—if you pick up a bottle for this recipe and have some left over, enjoy it over ice in the afternoon.

1 ounce gin

¾ ounce Cointreau

¾ ounce Cocchi Americano

¾ ounce fresh lemon juice

Absinthe, to rinse the glass

Coat the inside of a chilled cocktail glass with absinthe. Shake ingredients with ice and strain into the prepared glass.

Producers: David Bowie, Iggy Pop, Colin Thurston   Label: RCA   33

THE CARS

1978   GENRE: ROCK, POWER POP, NEW WAVE   WHEN TO SPIN: NEW WAVE DANCE PARTY

LINER NOTES   WHEN THIS DEBUT ALBUM DROPPED IN 1978, IT BECAME AN INSTANT CLASSIC. THE MIX OF ENGINE-REVVING NEW WAVE AND HARD-DRIVING POP SONGS MADE LISTENERS WANT TO SIT A LITTLE LOWER IN THE DRIVER'S SEAT AND TAKE THE CURVES A LITTLE FASTER. GANGLY NERD RIC OCASEK DELIVERS HIS LYRICS WITH A KNOWING SNEER, LIFTING THE ALBUM BEYOND THE MAINSTREAM TO THE PERENNIALLY COOL. GET READY TO LET THE GOOD TIMES ROLL.

BEFORE YOU DROP THE NEEDLE   THINK OF THIS AS A HIGH-ENERGY PARTY ALBUM THAT WILL GET HANDS CLAPPING. IT'S PERFECT FOR A NIGHT OF RETRO VIDEO GAMING OR POKER.

GIN AND IT

Simple, cool, to the point. The gin you know, and the "it" is sweet Italian vermouth. Popular in England, this classic is long overdue for its American adoption. We love this drink's elegance and simplicity, not to mention flavor. Traditionally, it's consumed at room temperature without ice. But that is gross, so we Americanize it by pouring it over a few jolly cubes.

2 ounces gin

1 ounce sweet vermouth

Combine ingredients in a rocks glass with two or three ice cubes.

CAR DRIVER

This is a great nonalcoholic drink for your designated D. It's not too sweet, and it has a nice fizz from the ginger ale (we like to use ginger beer, which has a little more kick). Of course, if you want to top it off with booze, be our guest.

2 ounces fresh pineapple juice

1 ounce fresh lemon juice

$\frac{1}{2}$ ounce grenadine (recipe, page 212)

2 ounces ginger ale

Lemon wedge, for garnish

Shake all ingredients except ginger ale and pour into a chilled rocks glass filled with ice. Top with ginger ale and garnish with a lemon wedge.

Producer: Roy Thomas Baker   Label: AIR Studios

LONDON CALLING
THE CLASH

1979
Genre: Post-Punk, Rock, Ska, Reggae, Rockabilly
When to Spin: Toast the end of the world, or New Year's Eve

LINER NOTES Primal and political, the Clash's third studio album is a stylistic mashup of various genres all pulled together with the force of a hurricane. The record is perhaps the apex of the band's creative output. As a rebellious call to storm the streets, full of angsty howls, screeches, and blasting guitar, the force of this album's apocalyptic spirit is uncontainable. It evokes the twilight of civilization, so meet the end of the world with style and aplomb—and a G&T.

BEFORE YOU DROP THE NEEDLE Ring in the New Year with vim and vigor, why don't you? Throw a Clash party and encourage everyone to toss their cares into a bonfire.

GIN AND TONIC

For a proper G&T, use a British gin. Beefeater or Plymouth always work well. Try Plymouth with lemon instead of lime, which is how it's served at the distillery in southern England. Novel.

2 ounces gin
3 ounces tonic water
Lime or lemon wedge, for garnish

Fill a rocks glass with ice. Add gin, top with tonic. Stir briefly, then garnish.

END OF THE WORLD

Do be careful not to make this the end of your night. Too many of these cocktail shots can result in your own personal Armageddon.

½ ounce high-proof rum
½ ounce whiskey
½ ounce vodka

Combine ingredients in a shot glass. Serve at room temperature without garnish, because the end of the world is no joke.

36

Producers: Guy Stevens, Mick Jones   Label: Epic

Unknown Pleasures
JOY DIVISION

1979
GENRE: Post-Punk, Goth
WHEN TO SPIN: Goth picnic

LINER NOTES   Grave, doleful, and lugubrious, Joy Division's first album captures the gray-tone feel of postindustrial wasteland Manchester, England—and sets it ablaze. The album boils over with mesmeric goth-meets-punk darkness. While carving out a similar hypnotic space as the Doors (page 177), Joy Division's sound is harsher and more urgent, all with an apocalyptic lilt. Epileptic lead singer Ian Curtis would be dead just a year later, and the band's—and album's—cult status assured.   **BEFORE YOU DROP THE NEEDLE**   Think dark: black tablecloths, black satin napkins, and—of course—plenty of chargrilled edibles!

PRODUCER: MARTIN HANNETT   LABEL: FACTORY

THE JOY DIVISION

A creation of bartender Phil Ward at the New York bar Death & Co., this drink is a Martini with added interest from citrus notes in the Cointreau as well as anise flavor from the absinthe. Both provide gothic depth. This is one of our favorite drinks and will be one of yours, too.

2 ounces London dry gin
1 ounce dry vermouth
½ ounce Cointreau
3 dashes absinthe
Lemon twist, for garnish

Stir ingredients with ice and strain into a cocktail glass.
Garnish with lemon twist.

DARK AND STORMY

A popular drink with British sailors at the turn of the twentieth century, today this cocktail is considered Bermuda's national libation (it's also trademarked by Gosling's). When mixing ginger beer and dark rum together, the result looks like storm clouds gathering on the horizon. It's beautiful to behold and mighty refreshing to sip.

2 ounces Gosling's Black Seal rum
3 ounces ginger beer
Lime wheel, for garnish
Candied ginger, for garnish (optional)

Fill a rocks glass with ice. Add rum and ginger beer, then stir.

1980 ⚡ **GENRE: HARD ROCK** ⚡ **WHEN TO SPIN: TOTAL RAGER**

LINER NOTES: This might be the apex of heavy metal, all grit and axe-smashing mayhem. The Australian band AC/DC's seventh album was recorded as a follow-up to their first internationally successful hit, "Highway to Hell." It featured newly hired front man Brian Johnson after the tragic death of former lead vocalist Bon Scott. Recorded in the Bahamas, the album focuses on standard rock 'n' roll themes cranked up to a deafening howl: sex, drinking, partying, and drugs. It went on to become one of the best-selling albums of all time, just behind Michael Jackson's *Thriller*.

BEFORE YOU DROP THE NEEDLE: Set up an AC/DC wet bar (see below).

BACK IN BLACK

HELL'S BELLS

Side A opens with church bells, so why not go full on AC/DC with this wildly easy, equal-parts party starter, aptly named after the first song?

1 ounce tequila
1 ounce black sambuca

Pour over ice into a rocks glass. Stir and serve.

AC/DC OPEN BAR

The song "Have a Drink on Me" mentions all of the booze below, including "cheap wine." To prepare an AC/DC wet bar, put out a bottle or two of each liquor along with a couple boxes of wine.

1 bottle whiskey
1 bottle gin
1 bottle brandy
1 bottle white lightning (moonshine)
1 bottle tequila
Cheap wine

ADDITIONAL MIXERS
Club soda
Tonic water
Coca-Cola
Lemon wedges
Lime wedges

Let guests make their own drinks and prepare for the party to shake all night long.

LICENSE

BEASTIE BOYS

TO ILL

1986

GENRE: HIP-HOP, ROCK   WHEN TO SPIN: SLACKER PARTY

LINER NOTES

License to III is full of both ridiculously bad rhymes and catchy creativity. Derisively labeled as "frat hip-hop" when it appeared, the album was ahead of its time—hilariously and offensively so—featuring rudimentary beats and vocals that are still just, well, stupid. But holding it to a high standard misses the point. The record appeared in the late '80s as a kind of canary-in-the-coal-mine warning for the slacker generation of the '90s that was to come. Today, it stands as a monument to giving zero f&*ks. And that is something that will always be refreshing.

BEFORE YOU DROP THE NEEDLE

Stock up on plenty of red Solo cups, but don't bother picking up your apartment.

SIDE A
BRASS MONKEY

Break out the drinking games! In the song "Brass Monkey," the B-boys reference the premade drink marketed and sold by Heublein from the '70s to the '90s, but you can make your own with malt liquor and OJ. To follow the spirit of this recipe, grab a 40-ounce bottle of Olde English, drink it to the top of the label, then add OJ. The recipe below is for, well, sharing.

8 ounces Olde English 800
4 ounces fresh orange juice

Mix ingredients together in a red Solo cup and enjoy.

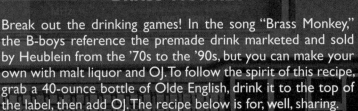

SIDE B
BROOKLYN

No sleep till . . . ! Not as well-known as its neighboring burrow's signature libation, the Manhattan, this cocktail is a forgotten classic in its own right. It's been a bit hard for the drink to come into full revival since the original recipe calls for Amer Picon, a French orange liqueur that is no longer readily available in the United States. But, by substituting an amaro like Torani Amer and adding a few dashes of orange bitters, you can approximate the flavor.

2 ounces rye whiskey
3/4 ounce dry vermouth
1/4 ounce Maraschino liqueur
1/4 ounce Torani Amer
4 dashes orange bitters

Stir ingredients with ice and strain into a chilled cocktail glass.

GUNS N' ROSES

APPETITE FOR DESTRUCTION

LINER NOTES Los Angeles glam band Guns N' Roses roared into the spotlight in the summer of 1987 with "Welcome to the Jungle" and "Paradise City" screaming to the top of the charts. One of the biggest debut albums ever, *Appetite for Destruction* gave the country a taste of sex, drugs, and rock 'n' roll at a time when the mainstream was caught up in nostalgic Reagan-era puritanism. This was a true blast of visceral id, and featured a faster and even less refined punk aesthetic than other hair bands of the late '80s. The album is perfect for karaoke or a dress-up hair band party.

BEFORE YOU DROP THE NEEDLE Notice that the two sides of this album are labeled "G" and "R" instead of Side A and Side B. Yeah. Time to break out your ripped G&R T-shirt, throw on a bandanna, and start fist pumpin'.

KAMIKAZE

A popular shot during the '80s, you can also serve this up in a cocktail glass. But why would you? Interesting fact: this is the drink that spawned the Cosmo—just add cranberry juice. Pinkies out, rock 'n' rollers!

1 ounce vodka
¾ ounce triple sec
¾ ounce fresh lime juice

**Shake ingredients with ice
and strain into a shot glass.**

RATTLE SKULL

A popular colonial drink that packs a wallop, this cocktail comes straight at you from revolutionary times to help woo that sweet child. Why chase your beer with a shot when you can just have them together? That's the early-American logic of this drink that is hard to refute. Try it over ice or without—the taste is similar to a Cuba Libre (rum and Coke).

12 ounces porter
1½ ounces rum or brandy
¾ ounce fresh lime juice
½ ounce brown sugar syrup
(1:1 sugar to water)

Add ingredients to a chilled beer mug and stir.

ODELAY

1996

BECK

Genre: Alternative Rock, Anti-Folk, Country, Noise Rock, Alt Hip-Hop
When to Spin: Arty pajama party

LINER NOTES

A musically innovative blend of rock, hip-hop, and folk with a connecting Americana thread, this is the album where Beck stepped beyond his hit single "Loser" and into the spotlight as a star. More than a poster child for the slacker generation, this album launched him as a serious musician able to bend genres and weave a coherent story over a full-length album. It stands as one of the great recordings of the '90s, and one of the most daring. Get down with hit after hit, as if you've just stuffed a dusty bar jukebox in space and it's spitting out constant unknown wonders.

BEFORE YOU DROP THE NEEDLE

Set out the paints and colored pencils, or, better yet, modeling clay.

MATADOR

Think of this as the margarita's wild cousin. The one that wore crazy clothes, got out of town and, against all odds, became successful. Acquiring fresh pineapple juice can be a pain but is worth the extra effort if you have a juicer or a juice bar nearby.

1½ ounces tequila

3 ounces fresh pineapple juice

1 tablespoon lime juice

Pineapple wedge, for garnish

Shake ingredients with ice. Strain into a Champagne flute or cocktail glass. Garnish with a pineapple wedge.

TEQUILA NEGRONI

Swapping tequila for gin in a Negroni makes for a tasty twist. Sometimes called an Agavoni (agave + negroni), the combination is typically made with equal parts tequila, Campari, and vermouth. But we like to "ladder" the ingredients so the bold flavors are better balanced. Be sure to use only 100 percent agave blanco or silver tequila for the best taste.

1½ ounces tequila

1 ounce sweet vermouth

¾ ounce Campari

2 dashes orange bitters

Grapefruit peel, for garnish

Stir the ingredients with ice and strain into a chilled rocks glass over ice. Garnish with a grapefruit peel.

PRODUCERS: Beck Hansen, The Dust Brothers, Mario Caldato Jr., Brian Paulson, Tom Rothrock, Rob Schnapf

LABEL: DGC

WHITE BLOOD CELLS

The album that launched Detroit duo Jack and Meg White to commercial success, this LP (their third studio album) offers a rollicking rock 'n' roll ride of unapologetic guitars and great songwriting. Recorded in less than four days, the record feels raw and uncut, capturing the band's live energy. The un-self-conscious, straightforward rocking makes *White Blood Cells* a great accompaniment to good whiskey, preferably bourbon or rye.

Invite a small group of friends over and ask each person to bring a bottle of hooch.

SIDE A WHISKEY SANGAREE

This is an old cocktail that is beautiful to behold and tasty to sip. We think it pairs perfectly with this album's glorious embodiment of all that is great about gritty rock 'n' roll. While the drink is the precursor to sangria, it maintains its growl.

2 OUNCES WHISKEY
½ TEASPOON DEMERARA SUGAR
1 TEASPOON WATER
2 TO 3 OUNCES CLUB SODA
½ OUNCE RUBY PORT

Combine whiskey, sugar, and water in a rocks glass and stir until sugar is combined. Fill glass with ice and top with club soda. Float port on top.

SIDE B WHISKEY TASTING (SEE PAGE 52)

THE WHITE STRIPES

HOW TO HOST A WHISKEY TASTING

WHAT YOU'LL NEED

Pencils | Plain white paper (one piece for each guest) | **Pitcher(s) of water** | **Tasting glasses** (or any low glasses with wide mouths) | **Brown lunch bags** (if you're going to blind-taste)

Ask each of your best booze-loving friends to bring a different bottle of whiskey to your abode for a night of evaluating spirits like a pro. If you hone your basic tasting abilities, you'll not only know good hooch from bad, but you'll know when a product exhibits quality—even if you do not like it. And that, friends, is true palate maturity and qualifies you to have opinions.

PREP STEPS

1. Provide each guest with a pencil, white paper, and as much glassware as you can muster. Ideally, you'll have three to four glasses at each seat so participants can compare bottles simultaneously. Make sure each participant has access to a pitcher of water.

2. Bag and number bottles if you are conducting the tasting blind. (We like to have everyone hand their bottles privately to the host so no one can see the labels.)

3. Pour everyone 1-ounce samples for however many glasses you have—i.e., pour the first three bottles if each participant has three glasses.

4. Explain the ranking categories for awarding medals, which are thus:

Gold: a bottle I would keep and covet in my own bar

Silver: a bottle I would give as a gift to a friend

Bronze: a bottle I would buy off the shelf

5. Remind participants that they are required to rank everything they taste.

Producer: Jack White   Label: Sympathy for the Record Industry

EVALUATION STEPS

1. Hold up a piece of white paper behind the first glass and jot down what the liquid looks like. It may be clear/colorless or it may be an ambrosial burnt-umber, reminiscent of Bob Ross's best lonely farmhouse bathed in autumnal sunlight. Whatever it is, it tells you a lot about what you're about to sip.

2. Next, "the nose." If you're nosing a whiskey, give it a sniff with your mouth open. Inhale through both your mouth and your nose simultaneously. If you're not getting much aroma because your glass is too deep, try covering the glass with a small plate, leaving it for a few seconds, removing the plate, and then smelling again. Whatever you do, try your hardest to get a sense of what's in the glass, and jot down whether it is pleasant and welcoming, or if it's flat or off-putting. Be guided by your nose. It will set your expectations.

3. First taste. Do not add water before your first or second taste. Give the liquid a sip and swish it around in your mouth—suck a little air into your mouth and sort of chew on the liquid. Yup, awkward. But try it anyway. If you're sipping whiskey, or say, mezcal, this first sip is going to snap your taste buds to attention and really whack them over the head. You may not taste much because your mouth is overwhelmed.

4. Wait forty-five seconds, and then take another sip. This time, your palate is more receptive and you can taste with more depth. The spirit will seem softer, and not as much of a shock to your tongue. Wild, right? The two sips forty-five seconds apart are really different. Take into account the liquid's viscosity—whether it is thin or thick and oily (the higher the proof, the thicker it feels). Then jot down the flavors you can decipher. There's no right answer here. Some flavors you might find are: oak, toffee, coffee, caramel, mint, curry, and anise.

5. Next, add a bit of water. A good rule of thumb is somewhere between 20 and 30 percent. In your remaining tasting liquid, that's just a few drops or less than a half a teaspoon. By lowering the ABV (alcohol by volume), especially with higher-proof liquors, more flavor notes will appear. What your tongue first perceived as merely hot and burning will now be mellowed enough to pick out a host of swirling nuances.

6. Write the flavors down. Look for depth. Look for complexity. Note the finish: Is it long or short? Are there any surprises between the aroma and the taste?

7. Whew, this was hard work. Now rank your bottles. It's important to hone your evaluative skills and decide—if you had to—which one of these you'd take to a desert island over others and why.

8. Duke it out. You all compare lists and argue it out until you agree (or agree to disagree) on the ranking of the bottles.

CHAPTER 2

DANCE

Party! Whether you're into disco or Gaga, this chapter calls all booty shakers to the dance floor. These albums will have you doing everything from an Irish jig with the Pogues (page 76) to the moonwalk with Michael Jackson's *Thriller* (page 68).

Prepare to lose yourself in tiki drinks with Talking Heads (page 66), get down with a Between the Sheets cocktail to Madonna (page 70), and sip an original creation from a legendary NYC hangout, Max's Kansas City, as you offer a few high kicks to Blondie's *Parallel Lines*.

Note that before you start springing around to Prince or James Brown, records do skip. A couple of tips: place your turntable on a wall shelf so it's not affected by floor vibrations, or set it on a heavy piece of furniture that will absorb the tectonics of those dancing feet. For a quick hack, use a couple of tennis balls as shock absorbers: just cut them in half and slide them under the corners of your player. Thennnn, roll out your bar cart, lower the lights, and shimmy.

LIVE AT THE

APOLLO

JAMES BROWN
AND THE FAMOUS FLAMES

APOLLO 1963

JAMES BROWN
AND THE FAMOUS FLAMES

GENRE: SOUL, R&B   WHEN TO SPIN: DANCE INSPIRATION

This LP captures twenty-seven minutes of the inimitable James Brown at his absolute prime. Remarkably, this is an entirely self-funded recording of a show on October 24, 1962, at the Apollo in Harlem, New York. It was a Wednesday night, chosen by Brown because that was normally amateur night and he knew the audience would be especially raucous. Brown's big bet paid off—the album was an instant hit, with radio stations around the country playing it in its entirety. *Live at the Apollo* has gone down in history as perhaps the best live performance ever captured on vinyl.

BEFORE YOU DROP THE NEEDLE

Pour drinks and get ready to spend the best half hour of your life channeling one of the greatest dancers of all time.

GODFATHER COCKTAIL

In honor of the "Godfather of Soul," as Brown is often called, this classy drink is a simple combination of Scotch and amaretto, with a lemon twist. If you sub vodka for the Scotch, it becomes a Godmother. Although it's not required, we think a little orange peel gives this cocktail needed lift, and, for a smoky treat, we love to add a bar spoon of Laphroaig. Note: the original was purportedly Marlon Brando's favorite drink.

1½ ounces Scotch

¾ ounce amaretto liqueur

1 bar spoon (1 teaspoon) Laphroaig (optional)

Orange peel, for garnish

Stir ingredients with ice and strain into a rocks glass filled with ice. Garnish with an orange peel.

NIGHT TRAIN

Don't die. No, really, don't say we didn't warn you. This is the drink that will have you waking up in another city with no pants and your wallet gone. But one or two? You will be dancing those pants off. Talk about energy. All aboard!

2 ounces espresso

1½ ounces vodka

1 ounce Frangelico

Shake ingredients with ice and strain into a chilled cocktail glass.

Producer: James Brown (original), Harry Weinger (Polydor reissue)   Label: King

SATURDAY NIGHT

FEVER

SOUNDTRACK

MULTIPLE ARTISTS

1977   GENRE: DISCO   WHEN TO SPIN: STUDIO 54 PARTY

Liner Notes: From the movie starring John Travolta, this soundtrack was a huge international sensation. Bringing the disco phenomenon to a mass audience, the album was composed mainly by the Bee Gees, who wrote much of it in a single weekend. One of only three soundtracks to ever earn a Grammy (the other two are *The Bodyguard* and *O Brother, Where Art Thou?*), this record is pure dance party. Don your leisure suits and get ready to boogie. Studio 54 in NYC was the place to be in the disco era, so channel your club vibes.

Before you drop the needle: **Hit the closest thrift store and invest in some polyester.**

HARVEY WALLBANGER

TOM COLLINS

In this popular drink from the '70s, Galliano's subtle and delicious vanilla and anise flavors really shine. Typically made with orange as the only juice, we add lemon for a bit more tartness. Note: replace vodka with tequila for a Freddy Fudpucker.

1½ ounces vodka
½ ounce Galliano
2 ounces fresh orange juice
¼ ounce fresh lemon juice
1 orange slice, for garnish

Shake ingredients with ice and strain into a chilled cocktail glass. Garnish with an orange slice.

This classic cocktail makes its appearance as early as the nineteenth century, and was a very popular drink from the get-go. Nearer to our era, it popped up in the '70s as a disco favorite. Light and refreshing, it's the ideal dance drink for those sweating it out in leisure suits and synthetic fabrics.

2 ounces gin
¾ ounce fresh lemon juice
¾ ounce simple syrup (page 213)
3 ounces club soda
Maraschino cherry, for garnish
Orange slice, for garnish

Shake gin, lemon juice, and simple syrup with ice and strain into a collins glass filled with ice. Top with club soda. To garnish, use a toothpick to thread the orange slice around the cherry.

BONUS TRACK

If you haven't seen *Saturday Night Fever*, make sure to watch it in advance, or project it on a wall as the album spins.

BLONDIE

PARALLEL LINES

1978

Genre
**New Wave,
Pop Rock**

When to Spin
Punk rock tea party

LINER NOTES

Hailed by critics as the perfect pop-rock album, Blondie's third recording launched the band to international fame with hit singles "One Way or Another" and "Heart of Glass." Leaving their post-punk sound for pure pop, the band still manages to keep some working-class grit between the candy-like melodies. More than anything, the album solidified lead singer Debbie Harry as a purring kitty-cat with vocal chops galore. For a girl who grew up fantasizing that she was the lost daughter of Marilyn Monroe, she emerges here as a dazzling blonde chanteuse herself.

BEFORE YOU DROP THE NEEDLE

Channel the punk rock tea party that Debbie Harry famously hosted at a London hotel in 1980 for other rocker dames, including Siouxsie Sioux (Siouxsie and the Banshees) and Chrissie Hynde (the Pretenders), among others—it's chronicled in the book *Negative*, published by Debbie Harry's then boyfriend and collaborator, Chris Stein.

GOLDEN CADILLAC

The NYC cool kids all hung out at Max's Kansas City, a restaurant and nightclub featuring drinks named after rockers. The first menu item read, "Blondie: A silky-smooth bombshell with Galliano, crème de cacao, and a good head." This inviting concoction is properly called a Golden Cadillac.

1 ounce Galliano
2 ounces white crème de cacao
1 ounce light cream

Shake ingredients with ice and strain into a chilled cocktail glass.

FRENCH BLONDE COCKTAIL

A tart and sweet combination to palpitate your heart of glass, this glamorous drink is a perennial party pleaser. If you don't have lemon bitters, which can be hard to come by, leave them out—the drink is still great without them.

1 ounce London dry gin
2 ounces Lillet Blanc
½ ounce St-Germain
2 dashes lemon bitters
2 ounces fresh grapefruit juice
Grapefruit peel, for garnish

Shake ingredients with ice. Strain into a cocktail glass. Garnish with a grapefruit peel.

MUNCHiES

PUNK ROCK TEA PARTY SANDWICHES

Invite your besties over for an afternoon of women in rock. Cue up Blondie, batch the cocktails (see note, page 215), prepare a big pot of black tea, then set out a tray or two of finger sandwiches. These four combinations pair particularly well with the Golden Cadillac (page 63) and the French Blonde (page 63), one of which is tart, the other sweet. Tea sandwiches are best served chilled.

FRESH GOAT CHEESE + LEMON ZEST + SLICED CUCUMBER

Mash about a teaspoon of lemon zest into fresh goat cheese (you may want to add a pinch of salt). Spread onto two slices of fresh white or wheat bread and press thinly sliced cucumber between them. Trim crusts and chill.

SMOKED TURKEY + CHEDDAR + SLICED RED APPLE + SAGE

Layer ingredients between two slices of white or wheat bread that has been lightly coated with mayonnaise. Or, serve on toasted baguette rounds, fanning the apple slices on top (brush with lemon to prevent browning), and sprinkle a tray of these with slivered sage.

LOX + CULTURED BUTTER + RADISH SPROUTS

Try this on pumpernickel party bread. Soften the butter to make it spreadable, then tuck sliced lox and a tuft of radish sprouts between slices. If you can't find radish sprouts, substitute fresh dill, sliced cucumber, watercress, or all three.

STRAWBERRY + RICOTTA + ORANGE FLOWER HONEY + MINT

Use slices of sweet bread or pound cake as a base for these open-faced tea sandwiches. Slather with ricotta, drizzle with honey, top with strawberry slices and chopped mint. You can also substitute fresh figs with a touch of orange zest.

REMAIN IN LIGHT

TALKING HEADS

GENRE

WHEN TO SPIN

NEW WAVE, FUNK, WORLD BEAT, EXPERIMENTAL ROCK

TIKI PARTY

1980

LINER NOTES

Merging multiple genres with tracks overlayed on top of looped African polyrhythms, the enduring appeal of the Talking Heads' fourth studio album (apart from its party-like listenability) is just how startlingly daring it was—and *still* sounds. The album's uniqueness and cohesion feel ecstatic and make for an incredible soundtrack to an eclectic gathering or BBQ. Its many cultural influences immediately evoke tiki, the postwar Polynesian cocktail moment that makes for an ideal liquid accompaniment to this creative band's magnum opus.

BEFORE YOU DROP THE NEEDLE

You'll need some tiki mugs and hurricane glasses, so hit the thrift stores or your grandparents' basement. Serve spicy food, like hot wings, along with fruit salad in carved-out melons or pineapples.

SIDE A   MAI TAI

The much maligned Mai Tai has sunk into a sad state at many tropical hotel bars, where it's often too sweet, but if made correctly it is one of the greatest drinks ever invented. The signature drink at Trader Vic's restaurants, this classic has been titillating palates since the 1940s. Orgeat, an almond syrup, can be purchased in liquor stores or online.

1 ounce dark rum
1 ounce amber rum
½ ounce orange curaçao
1 ounce fresh lime juice
¼ ounce orgeat
Lime wheel, for garnish
Mint sprig, for garnish

Shake ingredients with ice and strain into a rocks glass filled with ice. Garnish with lime and mint.

SIDE B   MISSIONARY'S DOWNFALL

One of the great garden-fresh cocktail creations of all time, this Don the Beachcomber masterpiece is so refreshing and light you'll wonder why it isn't as popular as, say, the daiquiri. This little number takes the blender party to a whole new level.

SERVES 2 (OR A LARGE DRINK FOR ONE)

2 ounces light rum
1 ounce peach brandy
2 ounces honey syrup
   (1:1 honey to water)
1 ounce fresh lime juice
½ cup diced fresh pineapple
¼ cup loosely packed mint leaves,
   plus a few sprigs, for garnish

Place ingredients in a blender with about 1 cup of ice. Divide into two chilled cocktail glasses and garnish with mint sprigs.

MUNCHIES!   TIKI PARTY MIX

This salty-sweet combination is terrific alongside rum drinks. Feel free to make it your own by adding or substituting the following: popcorn, dried mango or dried papaya, cashews, almonds, or a different mix of cereals or small crackers.

Preheat the oven to 300°F, and line a baking tray with parchment paper.
   Combine the first four ingredients in a large mixing bowl. In a small dish, combine melted coconut oil and spices. Pour the liquid over the mix, stir, then spread it onto the cookie sheet. Bake for 45 minutes, stirring every 15 minutes. Remove the cookie sheet from the oven and add dried pineapple, banana chips, and coconut. Mix with a large spoon. Cool party mix, then store it in a well-sealed container before serving.

2 cups Goldfish crackers
2 cups small pretzels
2 cups whole wheat Chex cereal
1 cup cashews or pecans
3 tablespoons coconut oil, melted
1 teaspoon chili powder
½ teaspoon ground cumin
1 cup dried pineapple, chopped
1 cup dried banana or plantain
   chips
½ cup toasted flaked coconut

Producer: Brian Eno   Label: Sire

Michael Jackson

THRILLER

1982

Genre:
Pop Rock, Post-Disco, Funk, R&B

When to Spin:
Halloween party

Liner Notes
No one who lived through the '80s can forget the electrifying performances of Michael Jackson, the Elvis of his era. Erotic and eccentric, his dance videos inspired every American teen to practice moonwalking across their shag-carpeted basement. *Thriller*, Jackson's sixth studio album, snagged an unheard-of eight Grammy Awards and surged up the charts to become the best-selling record of all time. Loaded with hit singles, this is the perfect album for a campy Halloween party or a glitter-filled '80s tribute night.

Before You Drop the Needle
Practice your dance moves and thrift some '80s clothes—the King of Pop was all about red leather jackets, white suits, sunglasses, and sparkle.

A ZOMBIE #2

Get the party started with this tiki classic from Trader Vic's. In a bit of marketing genius, the restaurant limited customers to two of these doozies. Of course, this only boosted sales. This is a serious rum bomb. Go crazy with the garnishes!

¾ ounce light rum

¾ ounce aged rum

½ ounce Grand Marnier

¼ ounce grenadine (see page 212)

1½ ounces fresh orange juice

2½ ounces fresh pineapple, cubed

1 ounce fresh lemon juice

½ ounce fresh lime juice

Blend ingredients with about 1 cup of ice. Serve with a straw in a chilled hurricane glass or tiki mug, if you wish.

B MOON WALK

We think Jackson deserves a classy Champagne drink, don't you? This recipe was created by Savoy Hotel bartender Joe Gilmore to commemorate Neil Armstrong's first steps on the moon. Moonwalk a tray of these to your friends?

1 ounce Grand Marnier

1 ounce fresh grapefruit juice

2 to 4 drops rose water

3½ ounces Champagne or other sparkling wine

Grapefruit peel, for garnish

Pour grapefruit juice, Grand Marnier, and a few careful drops of rose water into a Champagne flute. Stir, then top with bubbly. Garnish with a curl of grapefruit peel.

BONUS TRACK

Need some Halloween party inspo? Watch the Thriller video—it's full of zombies.

Producer: Quincy Jones   Label: Epic/CBS

MADONNA
LIKE A VIRGIN
1984

GENRE: POP **WHEN TO SPIN:** '80S DANCE PARTY

LINER NOTES Nothing says the '80s like the bustier-clad Madonna, who loved being a provocateur. Who can forget her performance at the 1984 MTV Music Video Awards, when she made every American parent seize up in their La-Z-Boy recliner by descending from a giant wedding cake and writhing around on the floor like a naughty chorus girl in heat? Batch some virgin drinks (or not) and raid your closet for something taboo, then get ready to sing along to some of the most simple yet seething lyrics around.

BEFORE YOU DROP THE NEEDLE Watch some Madonna videos, then hit the thrift stores for fingerless gloves, jean vests, bangles, and anything that says "stretch lace." Offer combs and hairspray to guests who need prodding to get into the spirit.

BETWEEN THE SHEETS

This suggestively named drink dates back to Prohibition, when it was thought that combining two different classes of liquors led to insta-inebriation. It doesn't, we've tried. But it is a thrilling flavor combination, and at a Madonna dance party the chance of finding oneself in bed is never far away.

1 ounce white rum

1 ounce Cognac

1 ounce Cointreau

½ ounce fresh lemon juice

Lemon twist, for garnish

Shake ingredients with ice and strain into a chilled cocktail glass. Garnish with a twist of lemon.

BEAUTY SPOT

All hail Madonna's signature cheek mark, a throwback to silver screen starlets. This cocktail was inspired by the film *The Artist* (2011), and created by Jen Marshall at Nighthawk Cinema in Brooklyn. Although the ingredients are similar to the classic Bijou (page 178), which calls for equal parts, this "laddered" drink makes for a deliciously balanced cocktail.

2 ounces gin

1 ounce sweet vermouth

½ ounce green Chartreuse

Orange twist, for garnish

Stir ingredients with ice and strain into a cocktail glass. Garnish with an orange twist.

Producers: Nile Rodgers, Madonna, Stephen Bray　　　Label: Sire

Prince
Purple Rain

1984   Genre: Pop, Funk, R&B

When to Spin: Cross-dressing party

LINER NOTES   Dearly beloved, we are gathered here today to listen to Prince's legendary soundtrack to his eponymous film, Purple Rain. It's time to get freaky as only a five-foot-two-inch, gender-bending, guitar-playing genius can. Let's not forget that this is a party album, which yielded five singles. Glam, industrial, and poppy all at once, the LP oozes with life and works as a bizarre autobiography (the film is loosely based on Prince's life in Minneapolis). Set out the purple bar napkins and adorn yourself with as many diamonds and pearls as you can. And frills, don't forget frills.

BEFORE YOU DROP THE NEEDLE   Raid the closet of your best friend of the opposite sex. Then kick off your inhibitions and have a helluva lot of fun.

Aviation

Take flight with this stunning purple drink! Originally created to celebrate early aviators Charles Lindbergh and Amelia Earhart, it fell into obscurity only to be brought roaring back by the recent craft cocktail resurgence. Crème Yvette can be substituted, but Crème de Violette is worth seeking out. We're willing to bet that this will become a cocktail staple in your repertoire.

1¾ ounces gin
¼ ounce Maraschino liqueur
1–2 teaspoons Crème de Violette
¾ ounce fresh lemon juice
¼ ounce simple syrup (page 213)
Lemon twist, for garnish

Shake ingredients with ice and strain into a chilled cocktail glass. Garnish with a lemon twist.

Fallen Angel

This cocktail comes by way of drinks writer Gary Regan, who in turn adapted it from the Drovers Tap Room in New York. Those recipes use Bacardí Limón, which we replicate with fresh lemon juice. It screams Prince, since it's lavender in color and full of bubbles.

1 ounce white rum
¼ ounce triple sec
¼ ounce cranberry juice
¼ ounce fresh lemon juice
1 ounce Champagne or other
    sparkling wine

Shake rum, triple sec, cranberry juice, and lemon juice with ice and strain into a chilled cocktail glass. Top with Champagne.

Producers: Prince and the Revolution   Label: Warner Bros.

LINER NOTES // Fancy a pint? Because a more raucous, danceable, booze-soaked album was never made. Grab your mates and prepare to fake your way through a sodden jig. Brimming with lively stories and steeped in history, the Pogues' second album is a winding cobblestone street of romance, politics, and compelling characters. Carving out their own sound between traditional music and rock, the record occupies its own universe—one where a slap on the back and another round are never far away. You'll be two-fisting by the end and never happier.

BEFORE YOU DROP THE NEEDLE // Go full-on Irish with all the tacky green trimmings, or cut the B.S. entirely—as the Pogues would have—and focus on flowing drinks.

SIDE A

SHOT OF JAMESON AND A HARP

A wee bit 'o the drop. Nothing says a night of dancing to Irish rock like shots of Jameson and bottles of Irish beer. Drink up, laddies.

1 shot Jameson
1 bottle Harp

Set the whiskey and beer side by side, and talk about the green, green grass of home.

SIDE B

TIPPERARY COCKTAIL

This classic is named after a town and a county in southern Ireland. It features Irish whiskey, of course, which is typically milder than other whiskeys—plus, a hit of bright green Chartreuse, an herbal liqueur.

2 ounces Irish whiskey
¾ ounce sweet vermouth
½ ounce green Chartreuse
Lemon twist, for garnish

Stir ingredients with ice and strain into a chilled cocktail glass. Garnish with a lemon twist.

RAISING HELL
RUN DMC

1986

LINER NOTES

This wasn't just the breakthrough record for Run-D.M.C., this was the album that demonstrated hip-hop was commercially viable and not a passing fad. Energetic, electric, and full of wicked rhymes, Run-D.M.C.'s ambition is matched only by a recording that stands as rap's first bona fide masterpiece, a total game changer that remains a perennial party starter. By the time the album hits the brilliant appropriation of Aerosmith's "Walk This Way," the drinks will be flowing, and by the end there may be underwear on the ceiling fan.

BEFORE YOU DROP THE NEEDLE

Make this the first album of the night. It never fails to get the ball rolling and guests chanting along.

THE PETER PIPER

Listen to the first song on Side A to get the reference, then enjoy this sour 'n' spicy number. It's adapted from a cocktail created by Alie Ward and Georgia Hardstark, hosts of the Cooking Channel's *Classy Ladies* show. Note: black pepper vodka is easy to make at home—we like to infuse our own by adding a couple tablespoons of black peppercorns to a bottle of vodka, then straining them out after about a week.

2 ounces pepper vodka
½ ounce pickle brine (from cornichons)
¼ ounce dry vermouth
2 cornichons

Stir vodka, brine, and vermouth with ice. Then strain into a chilled cocktail glass, and garnish with skewered pickles.

LITTLE DEVIL

From the great 1927 cocktail book by Harry McElhone, *Barflies and Cocktails*, comes this tasty little number created in London at Ciro's. It's a rather unique drink, more delicate than one might expect.

¾ ounce gin
¾ ounce white rum
½ ounce Cointreau
½ ounce lemon juice

Shake ingredients with ice, and strain into a chilled cocktail glass.

3 FEET HIGH AND RISING

DE LA SOUL 1989

GENRE Hip-Hop, Conscious Hip-Hop   **WHEN TO SPIN** Housewarming

LINER NOTES De La Soul's debut album features catchy, witty lyrics and a sweet groove that will put you in a great mood. A turn from the hip-hop clichés of guns, drugs, and women, the album instead builds on eclectic influences for a joyful ride through funny samples, Parliament-style funk, and African rhythms. The willingness to be playfully poppy paid off for the group, as the album became a major critical and commercial success, frequently appearing on best-albums-ever lists.

BEFORE YOU DROP THE NEEDLE Think of this album and the cocktails that go with it as a house blessing. Invite in (and drink up) the positive vibes.

SIDE A	SIDE B

CUPID COCKTAIL

A sherry shot that will put you in the mood and give you stamina (as egg cocktails are rumored to do), this drink has the velvety texture of love and goes down smooth. Don't be shy. Note: if this original recipe is too sweet, skip the powdered sugar.

2 ounces dry sherry (Oloroso)

1 whole small egg

1 teaspoon powdered sugar

Dash of cayenne pepper

Shake ingredients vigorously with ice and strain into a chilled cocktail glass.

FLAME OF LOVE

This storied drink hails from Chasen's in Los Angeles, long a favorite of the Hollywood set. It was created by bartender Pepe Ruiz for Dean Martin in 1970. The trick to flaming a peel is to cut several disks of orange peel and to express the oil from them toward the glass (not toward you). Bartenders use a match, but a lighter will be easier. The oil will flame up—it's a great magic show!

2 ounces vodka

¼ ounce fino sherry

3 orange peels, cut into coins

Coat the inside of a chilled cocktail glass with sherry, discarding any extra. Flame two peels into the glass one at a time, expressing flamed oil into the glass (discard peels). In a mixing glass, stir vodka with ice and strain into the prepared cocktail glass. Flame the third peel over the glass and use it as garnish.

Producers: Prince Paul, De La Soul   Label: Tommy Boy, Warner Bros.

LOW END THEORY

1991

GENRE: JAZZ RAP, ALTERNATIVE HIP-HOP

WHEN TO SPIN: CLASSY HOUSE PARTY

LINER NOTES

Pioneers of alternative hip-hop, Tribe's second studio album was one of the first to blend hip-hop with a chilled-out jazz vibe. The result is an album with great flow that includes classics like "Check the Rhime," "Jazz (We've Got)," and "Scenario." Profanity-free and dealing with social issues, the record features Q-Tip rhyming over legendary jazz player Ron Carter's bass lines. Smart, with a minimal sound that always emphasizes the downbeat, the result is a hypnotically fun ride that gets the head nodding and the body bouncing.

BEFORE YOU DROP THE NEEDLE

Drop the lights real low, and crank up the bass.

SIDE A QUEENS COCKTAIL

Tribe is from Queens, making this album a fine reason to drink one of five classic cocktails named after the boroughs of NYC. This combination most closely resembles its neighbor, the Bronx, which replaces the pineapple juice with OJ. Think of it as the original gin 'n' juice.

1½ ounces gin
¾ ounce sweet vermouth
¾ ounce dry vermouth
1 ounce fresh pineapple juice

Shake ingredients with ice and strain into a chilled cocktail glass.

SIDE B SIDECAR

Perhaps the signature drink of the great American Jazz Age, the Sidecar is a double-feature of two exceptional French products: Cognac (brandy) and Cointreau. With a sugared rim, it's a sure hit. And it's a swanky accompaniment to this uplifting, jazzy masterpiece.

2 ounces brandy
1 ounce Cointreau
¾ ounce fresh lemon juice
Sugar, to rim the glass
Orange peel, for garnish

Prepare a glass by wetting the rim and dipping it in sugar. Shake ingredients with ice and strain into the prepared glass. Garnish with an orange peel.

Producers: A Tribe Called Quest, Skeff Anselm   Label: Jive, RCA

BJÖRK
DEBUT

LINER NOTES   In first solo album after the dissolution of her group, the Sugarcubes, Björk left the sound of that band to explore an electronic landscape that infused jazz, trip hop, and house music with poppy, melodic songs. The results were one of the most distinctive and indefinable debuts of all time, a record that is a sensual, danceable feast. The album still sounds daring and groundbreaking, with a kind of naturalist Euro-trance meets Bollywood energy that never fails to set an incredible mood.   **BEFORE YOU DROP THE NEEDLE**   Celebrating the end of a breakup? Hanging out with your eccentric besties? It wouldn't be inappropriate to break out a Ouija board at some point during the night to channel "Venus as a Boy."

SIDE A — SWAN COCKTAIL

It was a major cultural moment when Björk appeared at the seventy-third Academy Awards (2001) boldly costumed as an avian creature. We honor it with this delicious cocktail that predates Prohibition (it appears in *Old Waldorf Bar Days*, 1931). A gorgeous little number, it deserves to be more popular than it is.

1½ ounces gin
¾ ounce dry vermouth
¼ ounce absinthe (or Pastis)
2 dashes Angostura bitters
½ ounce fresh lime juice
½ ounce simple syrup (page 213)

Shake ingredients with ice and strain into a chilled cocktail glass.

SIDE B — LONG HAPPINESS

Muddle your way through the beginning of Side B, then enjoy this delightfully fruity beer cocktail to "Violently Happy," the second-to-last song.

1½ ounces vodka
½ ounce gin
1 slice peeled ginger
1 tablespoon diced pineapple
2 ounces apple juice
2 ounces lager

Muddle ginger and pineapple in the bottom of a shaker. Add ice and liquids. Shake, then strain into an ice-filled collins glass. Serve with a straw.

BONUS TRACK

Look up the story of Björk's swan dress at the Academy Awards. True fact: she brought six ostrich eggs with her and "laid" them on the red carpet. The dress was later featured at the Museum of Modern Art (MoMA).

Producers: Nellee Hooper, Björk   Label: One Little Indian, Elektra

THE MISEDUCATION OF
LAURYN HILL

1998

GENRE:
**Hip-Hop, R&B,
Neo Soul, Reggae**

WHEN TO SPIN:
Spring fling

LINER NOTES After touring with the Fugees and becoming pregnant, Lauryn Hill was inspired to record a solo album that propelled her to international stardom. Blending elements from hip-hop, soul, R&B, and reggae, the album uses the Bible as inspiration, but weaves its story from a uniquely female point of view—and with a refreshing blend of confidence and vulnerability that marks the album's genius. Hill, who composed for Whitney Houston and spent time with Aretha Franklin, delivers one of the most urgent yet joyful recordings ever made. It sounds as true to its gospel roots today as it did two decades ago.

BEFORE YOU DROP THE NEEDLE There's something so upbeat about this album, it makes you want to drink bright sparkles. Toss it on the turntable when you need a pick-me-up.

SIDE A

WHITE SANGRIA WITH MELON BALLS AND MINT

Channel the happy vibe with this colorful sangria. A mix of melons (pink, orange, and green) looks crazy festive, but you can also simplify this with one or two melons.

4 ounces Calvados or pisco
1 bottle (750 ml) moscato wine, chilled
2 to 4 tablespoons honey, adjust to taste
1 lime, juiced
3 cups mixed melon balls (watermelon, canta-
    loupe, honeydew)
12 ounces sparkling water, chilled
Mint leaves, for garnish
Lime slices, for garnish

Combine honey, Calvados, lime juice, and melon balls in a large pitcher and refrigerate for an hour. Add the moscato and adjust taste if necessary (it will be sweet and strong before you add the sparkling water). Add water, garnish, and serve.

SIDE B

HOLY WATER

Hill's faith infuses this album with a hands-in the-air sense of hopefulness. Heck, she even named her child Zion and sings about his arrival in messianic terms. Stir up the holy water! Note that this makes a large drink.

2 ounces vodka
1 ounce triple sec
1 ounce light rum
2 ounces tonic water
Dash of grenadine (page 212)

Combine vodka, triple sec, and rum in a collins glass over ice. Top with tonic water and add a dash of grenadine.

Producers: Lauryn Hill, Che Guevara, Vada Nobles   Label: Ruffhouse, Columbia

2009
Genre: Pop, Dance, Electronic
When to Spin: Photo-shoot dance party

LINER NOTES

A dark, hypnotic, and swirling blend of dance anthems and straightforward songwriting, Gaga's second album has it all. First, there's "Bad Romance," the single (and accompanying video) that assured Mother Monster's position as outré pop diva extraordinaire. But there's also the Freddie Mercury–inspired ballad "Speechless," and the ABBA-esque "Alejandro." An amorphous star who is by turns sugar pop, goth, animé, and robotic, Gaga toys with questions of character and fame all while tugging on heartstrings.

BEFORE YOU DROP THE NEEDLE

Invite the extreme fashionistas in your life to wear lace and black pleather. Set up your tripod, hang a white sheet against a wall, and encourage everyone to step out of character and into a crazy portrait. *Work it, work it!*

SIDE A BRANDY ALEJANDRO

We like to turn the classic Brandy Alexander into an Alejandro with a little spice. It's the perfect libation for a dance hit ("Alejandro" is the second song) with a well-known video that has serious homoerotic overtones. Olé!

1 ounce brandy
1 ounce dark crème de cacao
1 ounce heavy cream
Pinch of freshly grated nutmeg
Pinch of cayenne pepper

Shake brandy, crème de cacao, and cream with ice and strain into a chilled cocktail glass. Garnish with nutmeg and cayenne.

SIDE B LADY MACBETH

Like Lady Macbeth, Gaga is all fierce ambition without inhibition. A sparkling ruby-colored beverage seems like the perfect cocktail to have in hand as you cue up the last song and chant "show me your teeth."

2 ounces ruby port
4 ounces Champagne or other sparkling wine
Lemon twist, for garnish

In a chilled Champagne flute, add the port, then the bubbly. Twist the lemon peel over the drink and drop into the glass.

Producers: Ron Fair, Fernando Garibay, Tal Herzberg, Rodney "Darkchild" Jerkins, Lady Gaga, RedOne, Teddy Riley, Space Cowboy

Label: Interscope

What's better than bringing home some fresh vinyl finds and dropping them on the turntable throughout a lazy weekend afternoon? Invite your besties over, surrender yourself to the couch, pour some gorgeous drinks, and take turns flipping records. Who knows, maybe you'll fall in love during one of these chill sessions and graduate to the next chapter, Seduce.

This chapter is loaded with gloriously mellow vibes, ideal for backyard parties, poker nights, after-bars, or all-day lounging with BFFs. The cocktail pairings here are all about relaxed sips, from Margaritas (page 102) to Frosé—yes, a rosé slushy (page 105). Plus, you'll find one of our favorite hot drinks, Red Wine Hot Chocolate (page 122) paired with Pink Floyd's *The Dark Side of the Moon*.

Elvis   Robert Johnson   The Beatles   Aretha Franklin   The Velvet Underground   Johnny Cash
Simon & Garfunkel   Carole King   David Bowie   Pink Floyd   Tom Waits   Bob Dylan   Eagles   Jackson Browne
Hank Williams   Bob Marley and the Wailers   U2   R.E.M.   Nirvana   Snoop Doggy Dogg   Buena Vista Social Club
Neutral Milk Hotel   Lucinda Williams   Wilco   Interpol   Amy Winehouse   Vampire Weekend

1957

ELVIS'

CHRISTMAS ALBUM

Genre: *Rock, Christmas Music*   **When to Spin: *White elephant party***

LINER NOTES   Released in multiple forms over the years, Elvis's (spelled "Elvis'" on the actual album) fourth studio recording is among the best-selling Christmas albums ever in the United States, and it features the crooner singing "Blue Christmas," among other classic hits. All the panache and charm is here, the King's voice swaddling the listener like a warm holiday blanket. Hopefully, the snow is thick outside and there's mulled cider on the stove, along with a few stiff drinks to edge out the chill.

Before You Drop the Needle

Decorate cookies with glitter, and take turns swapping "white elephant" gifts—either a tacky gift under ten dollars or a regift. Elvis's favorite sandwich (grilled banana, peanut butter, and bacon) would not be out of place.

Side A ~ Mulled Cider

Nothing says holiday cheer with family and friends like something bubbling on the stovetop. When that something is brimming with spices and soon to get booze added to it, so much the better. Or, as they say, Hallelujah!

Serves 6 comfortably, or 4 thirsty wise men
   1 red apple
   1½ teaspoons whole cloves
   1 orange, sliced
   2 quarts apple cider
   ¼ cup light brown sugar
   1 teaspoon allspice
   8 ounces dark rum or whiskey
   Grated nutmeg, for garnish
   Cinnamon sticks, for garnish

Stud the apple with cloves. In a stockpot, combine the remaining ingredients, except rum and garnishes. Bring to a simmer over low heat and simmer for 10 minutes. Turn off the heat and add the rum. Ladle into mugs and garnish with nutmeg and a cinnamon stick.

Side B ~ Grasshopper

Like a mint shake for adults, this is a delicious version which adds brandy for a bit more luxurious flavor. It's your present to yourself.

   1 ounce brandy
   1 ounce green crème de menthe
   1 ounce white crème de cacao
   1½ ounces heavy cream
   Chocolate shavings, for garnish

Shake ingredients vigorously with ice, then strain into a chilled martini glass. Garnish with chocolate shavings.

VOL.II

ROBERT JOHNSON

KING OF THE DELTA BLUES SINGERS

LINER NOTES

Little is known about Johnson, who died at age twenty-seven in obscurity. Born in Mississippi, he made a career of playing in juke joints around Memphis and in Arkansas, although he did travel as far as Chicago, New York, and Texas. Oftentimes, he just played on street corners and in barbershops. Released by Columbia Records in 1961 from sessions in 1936 and 1937, this compilation is widely considered one of the greatest and most influential albums of all time. An advance copy went to a newly signed singer, Bob Dylan, who popularized Johnson's songs among the folk-bohemians of the '60s. Although he never experienced success in his lifetime, Johnson's songs have become immortal.

BEFORE YOU DROP THE NEEDLE

Set out your poker chips, your little bowls of snacks, and keep the bling to a minimum, except for a pack of new cards.

1961   GENRE: Blues, Delta Blues   WHEN TO SPIN: Poker night

SIDE A

MISSISSIPPI PUNCH

Not a lot is known about the origin of this fabulous drink, found in Jerry Thomas's *The Bon Vivant's Companion*. We do know that it combines our favorite food groups—rum, bourbon, and brandy—into one balanced meal.

- 1½ ounces light rum
- 1 ounce rye whiskey or bourbon
- 1 ounce brandy
- Dash of Angostura bitters
- ½ ounce fresh lemon juice
- ½ teaspoon demerara sugar

Shake ingredients with ice and strain into a collins glass filled with ice.

SIDE B

GREYHOUND

While the first printed recipe for this drink appears in Harry Craddock's famous *Savoy Cocktail Book* in 1930, a 1945 *Harper's* magazine article mentions that the drink was served in a popular restaurant chain, called Post House, located at bus terminals. No better drink for the great singer of the crossroads.

- 2 ounces vodka
- 4 ounces fresh grapefruit juice

Add ingredients to a glass filled with ice and stir.

Producer: Don Law (original), Frank Driggs (reissue)   Label: Columbia

BOOZY CHICKEN SANDWICHES WITH HONEY AND AVOCADO SLAW

Serves 4

FOR THE MARINATED CHICKEN

4 chicken breasts

1 (3-inch) knob ginger, peeled and grated

¼ cup molasses

1 tablespoon soy sauce

2 tablespoons vegetable oil

¼ cup dark rum

2 tablespoons lime juice

FOR THE SLAW

1 tablespoon white wine vinegar

1 tablespoon fresh lime juice

⅓ cup plain yogurt

1½ tablespoons honey

1 teaspoon ground cumin

1 small clove garlic, grated or minced

1 teaspoon salt

2 jalapeños, seeded, quartered lengthwise, and very thinly sliced

¼ cup green onion, thinly sliced

3 to 4 sprigs cilantro, minced (about 2 tablespoons)

1 small head cabbage, thinly sliced (about 4 cups)

Sea salt and black pepper, to taste

2 avocados, cut into medium-size chunks

Potato rolls or kaiser rolls

Marinated in rum and molasses, these southern-inspired chicken breasts are great for tossing on the grill. The recipe scales up easily, too, if you decide to host a bash. Be sure to serve these with Mississippi Punch (page 100).

FOR THE CHICKEN

Combine the marinade ingredients in a resealable plastic bag, then add the chicken and give it a good shake. Let the chicken marinate for at least 2 hours or overnight.

Grill over medium-high heat until the center temperature reaches 150°F.

FOR THE SLAW

In a large mixing bowl, combine vinegar, lime juice, yogurt, honey, ground cumin, garlic, and salt. Add jalapeños, green onion, cilantro, and cabbage. Stir to coat vegetables. Let the slaw rest in the refrigerator for at least a half hour. When ready to serve, add avocado and gently stir. Add more salt and pepper, to taste.

Serve sliders on toasted potato buns or kaiser rolls.

SGT. PEPPER'S LONELY HEARTS CLUB BAND

THE BEATLES

LINER NOTES   The Beatles' eighth studio album is credited with ushering in the era of the LP album format for popular music. Not wanting to be treated as just boy performers, the group decided to record under a fictional alias to jolt their audience and demonstrate artistic ambition. The result was a full-length record that showed popular music could be every bit as serious as classical and jazz. From beginning to end, it's a romping magnum opus. Other musicians followed suit, and the LP—and the idea that musicians had to record a full album—became the enduring pop platform.

BEFORE YOU DROP THE NEEDLE   This is a great album for adults and kids alike, so break out the lawn games, blow up the bouncy castle, and luxuriate on pillows under the trees. Sundresses and seersucker encouraged.

SIDE A   EAST INDIA COCKTAIL

With this incredible classic, we pay homage to the Beatles' meeting with the Maharishi in London in 1967. The band then famously traveled to visit the guru in India in '68. The first global cocktail, it is a suitably sunny and whimsical drink.

2 ounces brandy
½ ounce orange curaçao
½ teaspoon Maraschino liqueur
Dash of Angostura bitters
1½ ounces fresh pineapple juice
Freshly grated nutmeg, for garnish

Stir ingredients with ice and strain into a cocktail glass. Garnish with nutmeg.

SIDE B   MARGARITA

Lovely Rita, meter maid! The trick to making this much maligned cocktail is to use fresh lime juice. Death to sour mix!

2 ounces blanco or silver tequila
1 ounce Cointreau
1 ounce fresh lime juice
Salt, to rim the glass (optional)
Lime wedge, for garnish

Rim a rocks glass with salt. Then, fill the glass with ice. Shake ingredients with ice and strain into the prepared glass. Garnish with the lime wedge.

Producer: George Martin   Label: Capitol

ARETHA

I Never Loved a Man (The Way I Love You)

FRANKLIN

LINER NOTES Franklin recorded a number of albums for Columbia in the early '60s, but this debut on Atlantic Records made her the superstar we know. The very first track introduced audiences to her version of "Respect," which would not only become her signature song but an anthem for the women's rights and civil rights struggles of the late '60s. With this album, recorded at Muscle Shoals, famed R&B producer Jerry Wexler finally refocused Franklin from the showtune-singing generalist she had been with Columbia, to the gospel-laced, undisputed queen of soul. It's smooth, with an undercurrent of strength against adversity.

GENRE:
Soul, R&B

WHEN TO SPIN:
Ice cream soul-cial

BEFORE YOU DROP THE NEEDLE

Pick a hot night, put on some cool clothes, and give the blender a workout.

A

ICE CREAM FLIP

Sweet and fruity, this drink is as smooth and velvety as Aretha's voice singing "Soul Serenade." The egg can be omitted, but it makes this drink extra rich.

1 ounce brandy
½ ounce orange curaçao
½ ounce Maraschino liqueur
1 egg
1 scoop vanilla ice cream
Freshly grated nutmeg, for garnish

Combine all of the ingredients in a blender. Pour into a chilled cocktail glass, and garnish with nutmeg.

B

FROSÉ

This is the icy treat you never knew you needed. Once you try it, it will permanently enter your party repertoire. Easy, refreshing, and delicious—it's so good it demands RESPECT!

1 bottle (750 ml) dry rosé
¼ cup simple syrup (page 213)
Lemon peel, for garnish

Combine rosé and simple syrup in a 13 x 9-inch pan. Seal it well with plastic wrap and put it in the freezer. Stir the mixture with a fork every half hour for about 3 hours, or until frozen. Serve in wine glasses with a garnish of lemon peel.

PRODUCER: JERRY WEXLER   LABEL: ATLANTIC

THE VELVET UNDERGROUND & NICO

1967 // GENRE: ART ROCK, PSYCHEDELIC ROCK, GARAGE ROCK // WHEN TO SPIN: AFTER BAR

LINER NOTES

While the Brits were invading the music scene with their particular brand of pop-meets-blues, a New York band featuring a throaty German fashion model opened up new possibilities for a distinctly American sound—avant-garde, lo-fi, and gritty. Success was not immediate; the album barely cracked 30,000 in sales. But what it did not achieve in commercial success, it made up for in lasting influence. With its new sound and decidedly urban themes—drug abuse and prostitution—the Velvet Underground showed an obsession with street life and introspection, combined with musical experimentation and hypnotic rhythms. Financed by artist Andy Warhol, the album sports a now iconic cover image: a banana!

BEFORE YOU DROP THE NEEDLE

Dim the lights, tslip into a flowing caftan, and pull your musical instruments out of the hall closet. Bonus points for bongos and a xylophone.

SIDE A

MOONLIGHT COCKTAIL

Conjure the vibey party scene that the Velvet Underground so perfectly encompassed with a batch of this moon-colored juice, a vintage sipper from *The Savoy Cocktail Book*. This selection pays homage to Nico, who was referred to as a "moon-goddess" for her great beauty.

1 ounce gin
¼ ounce kirsch (or Maraschino liqueur)
1 ounce white wine
¾ ounce fresh grapefruit juice
Lemon peel, for garnish

Shake ingredients with ice and strain into a chilled cocktail glass or punch glass. Garnish with lemon peel.

SIDE B

MILK PUNCH (WITH COOKIES)

From the menu at Max's Kansas City, the famous Manhattan bar and restaurant that became home to New York's underground music scene, we offer you a classic milk punch. It's easily doubled or tripled (Max's offered it by the pitcher). Serve with oatmeal cookies, naturally.

2 ounces brandy or bourbon
½ cup whole milk
1 teaspoon powdered sugar
¼ teaspoon vanilla extract
Freshly grated nutmeg, for garnish

Shake ingredients with ice and strain into a chilled rocks glass or a wine glass filled with ice. Garnish with grated nutmeg.

Bonus Track

To check out Nico on camera, watch Federico Fellini's *La Dolce Vita* (1960) and Andy Warhol's *Chelsea Girls* (1966). She's as enigmatic in person as she sounds on this record.

1968

Johnny Cash

Johnny Cash At Folsom Prison

GENRE · COUNTRY FOLK ROCK · BLUES ROCK   WHEN TO SPIN · HOUSE ARREST

COLUMBIA

STEREO

LINER NOTES   Revitalizing Cash's career, this album was recorded live over two shows on January 13, 1968. Obsessed with prison songs and their underlying loneliness (Cash had attempted suicide at Nickajack Cave a few months earlier), what's striking is how comfortable Cash is during this performance. He's one of the inmates. And the songs are delivered raw and straight, with great humor. The whistles and claps of those in the crowd make this a true timepiece. Listen for the moment when Cash calls out the associate warden. Surreal.

BEFORE YOU DROP THE NEEDLE   One of two live albums in this book, it's truly one to be savored—take a seat on the couch and lean in to the speaker. Few albums capture a time and place so beautifully.

SIDE A

Suffering Bastard

We like to serve this drink in a tin cup. Or coffee mugs if you have them. Anything simple. It's a classic cocktail for the tormented. Note that some traditionalists serve this drink with Cognac, but for Cash you gotta use bourbon.

1 ounce bourbon
1 ounce gin
½ ounce fresh lime juice
½ ounce simple syrup (page 213)
Dash of Angostura bitters
4 ounces chilled ginger beer
Orange slice, for garnish

Add bourbon, gin, lime juice, simple syrup, and bitters to a rocks or collins glass filled with ice. Stir. Top with ginger beer and garnish with the orange slice.

SIDE B

Stone Fence

The drink Ethan Allen and his boys got drunk on before raiding Fort Ticonderoga, it doesn't get any more Americana than this blend. It brings together two things the colonists liked best and had in good supply: rum and hard cider.

2 ounces dark rum
4 ounces hard cider
Dash of Angostura bitters

Combine ingredients in a rocks glass filled with ice.

Producers: Bob Johnston (original), Bob Irwin (reissue)   Label: Columbia

Bridge Over Troubled Water

Simon & Garfunkel 1970

GENRE // folk rock   **WHEN TO SPIN** // drinks with old friends

LINER NOTES

All the harmonizing genius of these two singers are in this album, a combination of stunningly poetic lyrics and incredible melodies. By 1970, the singing troubadours Paul Simon and Art Garfunkel were stars. With their careers launched by the haunting classic "The Sound of Silence" in '65, they followed up with three hit albums. But *Bridge over Troubled Water* was to be their biggest success, and also their swan song. The duo broke up later the same year over artistic differences and Garfunkel's desire to pursue acting (his debut role was in 1970's *Catch-22*). Today, this album plays like the comforting soundtrack to a more innocent time, full of tenderness and hope. Cozy up and listen to it on the couch with your BFFs.

BEFORE YOU DROP THE NEEDLE

Light some candles, set out a box of tissues—this one can be a tearjerker.

Producers: Paul Simon, Art Garfunkel, Roy Halee   Label: Columbia

A

St. Cecilia Punch

This southern punch is one of our favorites. We promise it won't break your heart or your confidence. Besides accompanying this album, it's also festive to serve around the holidays.

Serves 8 to 12

6 ounces (¾ cup) dark rum
8 ounces (1 cup) brandy
3 medium lemons, sliced
¾ cup granulated sugar
2 green tea bags
½ pineapple, peeled, cored, sliced ½ inch thick, and cut into small wedges
1 bottle (750 ml) Champagne or other sparkling wine
6 cups (1.4 liters) sparkling water, chilled

Steep lemons in brandy at room temperature overnight. Combine sugar with ¾ cup water in a saucepan and bring to a boil, stirring occasionally until sugar dissolves. Remove from heat and add tea bags. Steep for 2 to 3 minutes, discard the tea bags, and let the syrup cool.

A few hours before serving, combine the lemons, brandy, syrup, rum, and pineapple in a large pitcher or bowl and chill in the refrigerator. To serve, transfer this mix to a punch bowl. Add the sparkling wine and sparkling water, and gently stir. Serve with a big block of ice.

B

Airmail

This cocktail tastes like a French 75 (see page 118) took a holiday in the Caribbean. As such, it's the ideal match to the song "Why Don't You Write Me," Paul Simon's first foray into reggae. You'll love its soft contours while listening to Art and Paul's dulcet tones.

1½ ounces gold rum
¾ ounce fresh lime juice
¾ ounce honey syrup (2:1 honey to water)
Champagne or other sparkling wine, to taste
Lime peel, for garnish

Shake ingredients, except Champagne, with ice and strain into a collins glass filled with ice. Top with Champagne and garnish with a lime peel.

Tapestry
Carole King

1971   Genre: Rock, Folk, Pop   When to Spin: Clothing swap

Spare and perfect, the songs on King's second studio album burrowed their way into your consciousness long before you knew who she was. They're just that good. Considered one of the greatest female solo albums of all time, King delivers a record that is accomplished, intimate, and sentimental, yet utterly entrancing. It's all the more testament to her writing skills and artistry that she can use her thin voice to convey such great range. This is an ideal rainy-day record. Take a cue from the album cover and curl up with your cat on a windowsill. Or, host a cozy gathering.

BEFORE YOU DROP THE NEEDLE

Invite your friends to bring over things they no longer wear. Drop them all into the middle of the floor and take turns fishing. When someone finds a perfect fit, make them another drink!

A

DREAMY DORINI SMOKING MARTINI

What could be more perfect than nursing a slightly smoky Martini to *Tapestry*'s title song? Invented by New York bartender Audrey Saunders, owner of Pegu Club, this sipper is sultry and mature. Pour yourself one on the couch and pull a wool blanket over your knees.

2 ounces vodka

½ ounce Laphroaig

6 drops Pernod

Lemon twist, for garnish

Stir ingredients and strain into a chilled cocktail glass. Garnish with lemon.

B

HOT TODDY

The Brits, while in India, used to consume a drink made from the fermented sap of the toddy palm, which is where this warm concoction gets its name. However, the classic hot version we know today most likely hails from Scotland, where it was made with—you guessed it— Scotch. In the Americas, we originally drank it with rum, although these days it's traditionally brandy or bourbon.

2 ounces brandy or bourbon

2 tablespoons honey

½ ounce fresh lemon juice

6 ounces hot water or black tea

1 thick-cut lemon wheel, for garnish

3 cloves, for garnish

Combine brandy, honey, and lemon juice in a warmed mug or pint glass. Top with water or tea. Stir. Drop in a lemon wheel pierced with 3 cloves.

DAVID BOWIE

The Rise and Fall of
ZIGGY STARDUST
and the Spiders from Mars

1972

Genre: Rock, Art Rock, Glam Rock

When to Spin: Glam night

LINER NOTES

This concept album tells the fictional story of a bisexual alien rock star named Ziggy Stardust. It was inspired by rocker Vince Taylor, who, after a breakdown, was convinced he was half-god/half-alien. Upon its release, this record generated controversy concerning the sexual ambiguity of its subject. Bowie originally conceived of the album as a soundtrack to a TV show, which accounts for some of its theatricality. With strong musical coherence and well-known songs like "Starman," "Suffragette City," and "Rock 'n' Roll Suicide," it's considered Bowie's greatest work.

BEFORE YOU DROP THE NEEDLE

Break out the body glitter, spike your hair, and feel free to explore some ambiguous couture. Then serve up this glorious pair of Champagne cocktails.

SIDE A : FRENCH 75

One of the most beautiful drinks in all of cocktail glam-dom, this lux libation combines lemony gin flavors with bubbles. Named after a French artillery gun that helped win World War I, it can be quite the bombshell. Serve it straight up or on the rocks.

1 ounce gin

½ ounce fresh lemon juice

½ ounce simple syrup (page 213)

4 ounces Champagne or other sparkling wine

Lemon peel, for garnish

Shake gin, lemon juice, and simple syrup with ice. Strain over ice into a collins glass. Top with Champagne and garnish with a lemon peel.

SIDE B : CHAMPAGNE CUP

Originally a punch filled with a variety of fruits, we like to make this into a single cocktail and let guests add their own garnishes. If you don't have Benedictine, or can't find it, Grand Marnier will do nicely. Garnish according to the season.

¾ ounce brandy

½ ounce Benedictine

Champagne or other sparkling wine, to top

Garnish options: mint, cucumber coins, brandied cherries, pineapple wedge

Combine brandy and Benedictine in a Champagne glass. Top with Champagne. Garnish as desired.

Producers: David Bowie, Ken Scott   Label: RCA

1973

THE DARK SIDE OF THE MOON

PINK FLOYD

GENRE: PROGRESSIVE ROCK, PSYCHEDELIC ROCK, SPACE ROCK   WHEN TO SPIN: SOLSTICE PARTY

LINER NOTES: Conceived by Roger Waters as an album that would concentrate on "things that made people mad," the eighth studio album by Pink Floyd is a sprawling work that deals with greed, mental illness, death, and the passage of time. It produced two singles, "Money" and "Us and Them," but stands better as a whole. Full of brooding and experimentation, the record offers a story arc, and has famously been paired as an unintentional soundtrack to *The Wizard of Oz* (try it, it works). Get comfortable, zone out, tune in—this is one of rock 'n' roll's most magnificent, dreamiest journeys.   BEFORE YOU DROP THE NEEDLE: Light candles, set some intentions, and make seasonally inspired snacks. Then pass around some smudge sticks and let everyone get clear before they get loopy.

RED WINE
HOT CHOCOLATE

ECLIPSE
COCKTAIL

We find that this album speaks to us most in either deep summer or deep winter. For those cold days that give you the winter blues, this concoction adapted from the blog *Yeah . . . ImmaEatThat* (immaeatthat.com) never fails to lift our spirits. It's the ultimate comfort drink to pair with this cinematic album. Tip: if you like a bit of spice, add a dash of ground chipotle on top.

A longtime favorite from the speakeasy bar PDT in New York, this drink was inspired by ancient Aztecs who served fermented agave to their victims before sacrificing them to the gods. Sounds like a rockin' solstice party to us. Also, if you're worried about buying the fairly obscure Cherry Heering, remember that it's used in the classic Blood and Sand (page 180). You'll consume that bottle faster than you think.

Serves 2 to 4

1^1/$_2$ cups whole milk

^{1}/$_3$ cup semisweet chocolate chips

^{3}/$_4$ cup red wine

2 ounces El Tesoro Anejo Tequila
   (as specified by the original recipe)

^{3}/$_4$ ounce Aperol

^{3}/$_4$ ounce Cherry Heering

^{3}/$_4$ ounce lemon Juice

Mezcal, for rinsing the glass

Lemon twist, for garnish

In a saucepan over medium heat, combine milk and chocolate chips. Whisk continuously until chocolate is melted. Do not boil. Add red wine, stir, and heat until warm. Pour into mugs and serve.

Coat the inside of a chilled cocktail glass with mezcal, discarding any extra. Shake remaining ingredients with ice and strain into the prepared glass. Garnish with the lemon twist.

ASTRAL SALAD WITH PURPLE GODDESS DRESSING

Two things inspired us here: Pink Floyd's iconic album cover with its rainbow-colored prism and founder Syd Barrett's love of gardening—something he reputedly turned to after he left the band in 1968 (he was not part of this recording, though several songs were dedicated to him). In addition to the "astral elements" here, like kiwi moons and cucumber swirls, feel free to add edible flowers and stars cut from radishes.

FOR SALAD

1 package (5-ounce) mixed greens
1 cup finely sliced purple cabbage
1 peeled, seedless cucumber, shaved into ribbons
1 package (6-ounce) blueberries (or strawberries)
1 pomegranate, seeds only
1 small orange, peeled and sectioned
2 kiwis, sliced and halved
1/2 cup cashews
Zest of 1 lemon
1 sprig purple basil, leaves only

FOR PURPLE BASIL DRESSING

4 sprigs purple basil
1 cup Greek yogurt
1 small shallot
2 teaspoons fresh lemon juice
1 teaspoon sea salt
2 tablespoons extra virgin olive oil

FOR THE SALAD

In a wide salad bowl or on a large platter, combine the mixed greens and purple cabbage. Arrange on top: coils of ribboned cucumber, berries, pomegranate seeds, orange sections (these look prettiest if you remove the membrane), kiwi moons, and cashews. Garnish with lemon zest and purple basil leaves.

FOR THE DRESSING

Place all of the ingredients into a blender and puree until smooth. Serve the dressing in a bowl on the side.

TOM WAITS   CLOSING TIME

1973

Genre:
Rock, Blues, Jazz, Folk

When to Spin:
Midnight breakfast

LINER NOTES

Filled with emotion and melancholy, Tom Waits's debut album is like sifting through a box of old sepia-tone photos. There's nostalgia, heartache, and forgotten moments rediscovered. Channeling the loneliness of bar close, this masterpiece appeared with little fanfare but has since been reissued multiple times and achieved cult status. An intimate piano-jazz album that skews folk, this is one to nurse old wounds or collect your thoughts by. Take a tug off the bottle and pass. It's a testament to this album's enduring power that Waits's lullabies can be used to exorcise your ghosts, woo a new lover, or rock a newborn to sleep.

BEFORE YOU DROP THE NEEDLE

Fry some eggs and drop some bread into the toaster. This is a great late-night album, as it calls to mind an old piano bar/coffee-house from another era.

SIDE A OLD FASHIONED

This may be the ultimate brown liquor album, so it's fitting that it be paired with the original cocktail, the one from which all others sprang. Make a simple, classic version (no fruit). The drink may have developed as early as the late 1700s, and we imagine it gets its name from old-timers coming into the bar and ordering a drink "the old-fashioned" way.

2 ounces whiskey or brandy
2 to 3 dashes of
  Angostura bitters
1 demerara sugar cube
1 teaspoon water
Orange peel, for garnish

Muddle sugar cube, bitters, and water in a chilled rocks glass. Fill glass with ice and add whiskey. Garnish with an orange peel.

SIDE B JAMO AND GINGER

The second side opens with "Rosie," a song that will melt the ice in your veins. And nothing will make sense except a final whiskey and ginger by the light of the stereo. Any whiskey will do, but good old Jameson is right.

1½ ounces whiskey
4 ounces ginger beer
Lime wedge (optional)

Combine whiskey and ginger beer on ice in a rocks glass. Squeeze in a lime wedge, if you desire.

Producer: Jerry Yester   Label: Asylum

BLOOD ON THE TRACKS

BOB DYLAN 1975

GENRE: Rock, Folk   **WHEN TO SPIN:** Sunday afternoon hangout

Liner Notes

A major comeback, *Blood on the Tracks* is often considered an autobiographical album about Dylan's breakup with his wife, Sara. And while this has been confirmed by his son, Jakob, Dylan maintains that the songs were based on Chekhov short stories. *Mmmkay.* Regardless, the album is a mature work and deeply confessional. Certainly, for story-seekers and -tellers, this is the recording *non plus ultra*.

Before You Drop the Needle

Dylan and chillin' require little explanation. Start a pot of soup (page 181) and laze around, or take a nap on a sunlit patch of carpet.

A: New York Sour

A whiskey sour with a wine float, this cocktail is beautiful to behold. It's both sophisticated and earthy, a marriage of wine and rye. Armed with both, it is easier to face life's existential sorrows.

2 ounces rye whiskey or bourbon

1 ounce fresh lemon juice

$1/2$ ounce simple syrup (page 213)

$1/2$ ounce red wine, to float

Lemon wheel, for garnish

Cherry, for garnish

Shake whiskey, lemon juice, and simple syrup with ice and strain into a rocks glass over ice. Float wine on top. For the garnish, use a bamboo skewer or toothpick to thread a lemon wheel around a cherry.

B: Beers Knees

A riff on the classic Prohibition-era cocktail, the Bee's Knees, this tasty blend of gin and wheat beer makes for a light quaffer. Its golden glow will pull you toward the light. Plus, it's a crowd pleaser, loved by all.

$1^1/2$ ounces gin

1 ounce fresh lemon juice

1 ounce honey syrup (1:1 honey to water)

3 ounces Hefeweizen

Lemon wedge, for garnish

Shake gin, lemon juice, and honey syrup with ice and strain into a collins glass filled with ice. Top with Hefeweizen. Garnish with lemon.

Hotel
California
EAGLES

LINER NOTES

The Eagles' fifth recording is a concept album centered on the themes of ruined paradise, innocence lost, and the excesses and decadence of late '70s Los Angeles. While the record's subject is the decline of America, musically it is a soft statement—beautiful melodies are set to easily digestible beats and even a relaxing Caribbean lilt. Occasionally profound lyrics and a cohesive feel make this not only one of rock's greatest albums, but also one of the most listenable. And timing a first drink with the title track's epic guitar solo makes for the perfect reverie.

BEFORE YOU DROP THE NEEDLE

Let your hair go beachy, get out your mandala blankets, and hang a few lanterns in the trees. Then break out the summer drinks and sit around the fire.

BEACHCOMBER COCKTAIL

Think of this classic tiki drink as something like a Maraschino-flavored Daiquiri. Because, while there's only a touch of the liqueur, it does come through, making for a wonderfully cherry-kissed libation. This is a variation of the original recipe from *Trader Vic's Bartender's Guide*, printed in 1947. It can be shaken and strained, or blended with about a cup of ice.

2 ounces white rum

¾ ounce Cointreau

¾ ounce fresh lime juice

½ teaspoon Maraschino liqueur

Blend ingredients with about 1 cup of ice and pour into a chilled cocktail glass.

MOJITO

Born in Havana, Cuba—although the date and origin are contested and it could be as old as the 1500s—this classic cocktail gained popularity as a Hemingway favorite after World War II. It has gone on to become one of the most ordered drinks at bars, to the chagrin of many a tired muddler. Simple and refreshing, it is a great drink to serve at parties.

2 ounces white rum

6 mint leaves, plus a sprig

¾ ounce simple syrup (page 213)

¾ ounce fresh lime juice

2 ounces club soda

In a rocks glass, muddle mint leaves with simple syrup. Add rum and lime juice. Stir. Fill the glass with ice and top with club soda. Garnish with a sprig of mint.

Producer: Bill Szymczyk   Label: Asylum

Running on Empty
Jackson Browne

1977   Genre: Rock, Folk, Country Rock   When to Spin: Travel planning

LINER NOTES The ultimate road album, Jackson Browne's melancholic *Running on Empty* was recorded entirely on his tour bus, in hotels, or live onstage. Working from new material, Browne created an album that brought his easy California vibe and boyish face to the forefront of American pop. With a shifting mix of unplugged folk rock and groovy electric guitar, this is the album you want to hear on a rainy night when you feel pangs of love or regret. Drop the needle, pour yourself a drink, and sketch out your next road trip.

SIDE A   SIDE B

OLD PAL

Similar to a Negroni, the Old Pal is a hard-hitting three-ingredient cocktail that would have been easy enough to fix while on tour. It's a stiff old-school sipper that has made a comeback since it first appeared in the '20s, showing up in the 1927 edition of Harry MacElhone's *Harry's ABC of Mixing Cocktails*. Ahhh, the bittersweet comfort of Campari and rye. Few remedies for heartache are better than curling up on the couch with an Old Pal.

- 1 ounce rye whiskey

- 1 ounce Campari

- 1 ounce dry vermouth

- Orange peel or lemon peel, to garnish

Stir the ingredients, then strain into a chilled cocktail glass. Garnish with orange or lemon peel.

WHITE PLUSH

We aren't going to lie: *Running on Empty* is a lonesome album, full of one-night stands, cocaine, and pleading. Fortify yourself for the second side with this stunning stomach-coating cooler. There are several recipes for a White Plush, but our favorite is this one, made from ingredients that can easily be stored in a hotel mini fridge.

- 1½ ounces blended Scotch

- ½ cup whole milk

- ½ teaspoon powdered sugar

Shake and strain into a rocks glass over a single large cube of ice.

Hank Williams

40 Greatest Hits

1978   Genre: Country, Blues   When to Spin: Front porch nap

LINER NOTES

Released on the twenty-fifth anniversary of Williams's death, this two-record album encompasses many of the songs that made the hard-drinking Williams famous. He was banned from the Grand Ole Opry and dead by twenty-nine, yet the cult hero's music is full of deep longing, with a somber resignation to a dissolute life. Although, for recordings full of heartache and gloom, there is also an indomitable spirit that springs from the itinerant hillbilly troubadour's voice. This is a perennial sing-along favorite that is sentimental and real.

BEFORE YOU DROP THE NEEDLE

Grab your rocking chairs and relax, preferably with a cowboy hat lowered over one eye.

SIDE A ← ❧ → SIDE B

BOURBON AND BRANCH

"Branch water" refers to water from a stream—ideally, you'd use the same water that fed into the distillery, an old practice and still a common term used in bars to refer to bourbon cut with water. While you probably wouldn't want to dip your tin cup in a creek nowadays, adding a splash of spring water to a glass of whiskey opens up the aromatics.

2 ounces bourbon

Splash of spring water

Pour bourbon into a Mason jar or tin cup, then add a little water.

SHANDY (IN A CAN)

Shandy is short for Shandygaff, a drink that rose to popularity in England in the 1800s. The drink screams (or yodels!) summer, and the combination of citrus and beer is the ultimate porch pounder. Refreshing and low in alcohol, it's the long listening session's best friend. Heck, make up a whole pitcher of the stuff and say, "Move it on over."

1 bottle lager

4 ounces lemonade

Lemon wheel, for garnish

Combine beer and lemonade in a tin can or pint glass, and stir. Garnish with a lemon wheel.

Producers: Fred Rose, Wesley Rose   Label: Mercury

Bob Marley
AND THE WAILERS

1984   GENRE: **REGGAE**   WHEN TO SPIN: **CHILLAX-A-THON**

LINER NOTES   The best-selling reggae album of all time, this record was released three years after Marley's death from cancer. Essentially a collection of his greatest hits and singles, *Legend* gathers together Marley's epic cry for hope and message of universal love. While the lyrics call for political action, the album is also one long ode to relaxation. Settle into the gentle rhythms and feel all right.

BEFORE YOU DROP THE NEEDLE   Bring out the lawn chairs and make like you're on island time.

LEGEND

PLANTER'S PUNCH

Sometimes called a Jamaican Rum Punch, the name and ingredient list for this classic drink vary wildly. See our recipe for grenadine on page 212, but do not fret if you're feeling lazy—this version works without it just as well.

2 ounces dark rum

Dash of Angostura bitters

1 ounce fresh pineapple juice

1 ounce fresh orange juice

1 ounce fresh lime juice

¼ ounce grenadine (page 212)

Lime wheel, for garnish

Orange wheel, for garnish

Shake ingredients with ice and strain into a rocks glass filled with ice. Garnish with lime and orange wheels.

JAMAICAN GUINNESS PUNCH

Rumored to be an aphrodisiac for men, this punch is a gloriously silky combination. The bitterness of the stout is perfectly rounded out by the sweetness of the condensed milk and given a lift with spice. This is the frothy beer shake of your dreams.

Serves 4

12 ounces Guinness or other stout

1 cup whole milk

¼ to ½ cup sweetened condensed milk

1 teaspoon vanilla extract

Freshly grated nutmeg, for garnish

Cinnamon, for garnish

In a blender, combine stout, milk, condensed milk, and vanilla with about 1 cup of ice and pulse for 8 to 10 seconds, or until well combined. Add more condensed milk if needed. Serve in a chilled rocks glass, garnished with nutmeg and cinnamon.

U2

GENRE // Rock, Alternative Rock   *WHEN TO SPIN* // Casual summer get-together

LINER NOTES

Beautiful and introspective with a sweeping yet minimalist feel, *The Joshua Tree* captures the gnarled image of the heroic twisted desert shrub to create a monumental album full of grace and resistance in the face of adversity. Produced by two legends, Brian Eno and Daniel Lanois, U2's fifth album centers on an American theme for the former punk-rock Irish band. U2 channeled the wide-open spaces they fell in love with while on tour across the United States, and the recording launched the group to superstardom.

BEFORE YOU DROP THE NEEDLE

Light the chiminea and break out the tequila. This is a great album for a bonfire.

1987

A
El Diablo

B
Desert Derby

Like a rare flower rising up from the California desert, the El Diablo pops with fragrance and color. First appearing in a Trader Vic's bar book in 1946, this ruby elixir makes for easy drinking and packs delicious flavor. Good ginger beer is key here.

1½ ounce reposado tequila
½ ounce crème de cassis
½ ounce fresh lime juice
2 to 3 ounces ginger beer
Lime wedge and a fresh blackberry, for garnish

Shake ingredients, except ginger beer, with ice. Strain into a collins glass filled with ice. Top with ginger beer. Skewer the lime wedge and berry for garnish.

The classic Brown Derby cocktail seems to have originated in Los Angeles. It is assumed to be named for the restaurant of the same name, although its creation is often credited to the nearby Vendome Club. A riff on the drink using a sage leaf appeared in *Bon Appétit* magazine back in 2014, and we base this drink on their idea. Whiskey loves grapefruit, and grapefruit and sage love each other—voilà, a flavor ménage à trois by association! It tastes like the desert and 'Merica.

2 ounces rye whiskey
2 dashes of Angostura bitters
1 ounce fresh red or pink grapefruit juice
½ ounce fresh lime juice
¼ ounce honey syrup (1:1 honey to water)
4 fresh sage leaves, divided

Shake ingredients with three of the sage leaves and strain into a chilled cocktail glass. Slap the final sage leaf between your palms to release its fragrance, then float the leaf on top of the drink.

PRODUCERS: DANIEL LANOIS, BRIAN ENO   LABEL: ISLAND

AUTOMATIC

R.E.M.

FOR THE PEOPLE

1992   GENRE: ALTERNATIVE ROCK   WHEN TO SPIN: LAZY SATURDAY

LINER NOTES WITH 1991'S OUT OF TIME, R.E.M. SWUNG FROM A COLLEGE BAND TO INTERNATIONAL STARDOM. WHEN THEY RETURNED TO THE STUDIO TO RECORD A FOLLOW-UP, THE BAND INTENDED TO MOVE AWAY FROM THE PREVIOUS ALBUM'S SOFTNESS TO SOMETHING HARDER. BUT OUT CAME THEIR SOFT MASTERPIECE. AND WHILE A QUIET ALBUM WITH A PERVASIVE MELANCHOLY WASN'T WHAT FANS EXPECTED, THE RECORDING WAS HUGELY SUCCESSFUL AND HAS BECOME AN ENDURING CLASSIC.   **BEFORE YOU DROP THE NEEDLE** WATER YOUR PLANTS, DON YOUR CARDIGAN, AND LIE DOWN TO LET THIS GENTLE AND DELICIOUS ALBUM WASH OVER YOU.

A: MINT JULEP   B: SAZERAC

The drink of Faulkner and the official cocktail of the Kentucky Derby, the Julep is a very old concoction indeed, and one of the first American drinks to achieve international fame. It originated in the southern colonies, where its first uses would have been medicinal.

2 ounces bourbon
½ ounce simple syrup (page 213)
6 mint leaves, plus three sprigs for garnish

Muddle mint and simple syrup in a rocks glass or Julep cup. Do not pulverize the mint, you only want to release its oils. Add crushed ice and bourbon, then stir until the cup frosts, about 30 seconds. Garnish with a few sprigs of mint and serve with a straw.

One of the great contemplative whiskey-based cocktails, the Sazerac sings of rye (or brandy) in perfect harmony with bitters and absinthe. It's a great sipper for music listening, and will warm you up should you go night swimming.

2 ounces rye whiskey or brandy
Absinthe, to coat the glass
Dash of Angostura bitters
4 dashes of Peychaud's bitters
1 sugar cube (or 1 teaspoon sugar)
Lemon peel, for garnish

Coat the inside of a rocks glass with absinthe. In a mixing glass, drop in the sugar cube, add the bitters and a splash of whiskey to help the sugar dissolve, then muddle. Add the remaining whiskey and stir with ice. Strain into the prepared rocks glass. Garnish with a lemon peel.

MTV UNPLUGGED IN NEW YORK

NIRVANA

1993 || GENRE: GRUNGE, ALTERNATIVE ROCK || WHEN TO SPIN: GRUNGE NIGHT

LINER NOTES   Nirvana broke out of the Northwest grunge rock scene with their hit "Smells Like Teen Spirit" on the 1991 album *Nevermind*. A runaway track that seemed to speak directly to and for a new generation, the band—and its leader, Kurt Cobain—became representative of the zeitgeist. Released just after Cobain's death, the "unplugged" MTV session is an utterly moving, delicate, and intimate recording, in stark contrast to the band's usual heavy sound and disaffection. During recording, Cobain was suffering from withdrawal and asked that the stage be set like a funeral—and what appears is a striking voice and vulnerability. Cobain, and Nirvana, revolutionized music. This is the album where you can hear why.

BEFORE YOU DROP THE NEEDLE   To embody the '90s grunge scene, wear a stocking cap, layered baggy clothes, and combat boots. Do not shower.

A – FLANNEL SHIRT

This is a cocktail from bartender and drinks writer Jeffrey Morgenthaler, from his bar Clyde Common in (where else?) Portland, Oregon. Northwest slacker central! There is a lot of flavor here. Don't be put off by the long list of ingredients—it's an amazing drink, and it's easy to batch for a crowd.

1¾ ounces Scotch
½ ounce Averna
½ teaspoon St. Elizabeth Allspice Dram
2 dashes of Angostura bitters
¼ ounce fresh lemon juice
1 teaspoon demerara syrup
   (2:1 demerara sugar to water)
1½ ounces apple cider
Orange peel, for garnish

Shake ingredients with ice and strain into a rocks glass filled with ice. Garnish with orange peel.

B – YORSH

Might as well just get this party rolling. Why waste your time in the slow lane drinking a ton of beers to get a buzz on when you can put the pedal down? It will not be said that you slacked on this one. This Russian (*of course*) concoction is an inspired shortcut.

2 ounces vodka
1 beer

Mix vodka and beer. Say something meaningful before you slug it.

SNOOP DOGGY DOGG

DOGGYSTYLE

1993   Genre: Gangsta Rap, G-Funk   When to Spin: Laid-back hot tub party

LINER NOTES Snoop Dogg had just come off working on Dr. Dre's landmark release, The Chronic, when he dove into the studio to record his debut. The album was a huge hit, and helped intro-duce West Coast hip-hop and G-funk to a mainstream audience. At turns brilliant and silly, with a great free-flowing vibe, the realist lyrics talk about guns, sex, cars, and money with a compelling straightforwardness that doesn't judge. As such, it's a party album that flies in the face of a heavy, gritty lifestyle.

BEFORE YOU DROP THE NEEDLE Wheel the bar cart out to the deck and crank up the bubbles so you can be splashin' along to the opening track ("Bathtub"). No other album says, "Will you give me a sponge bath?" like this one.

146

SIDE A GIN AND JUICE

Settle into this classic sipper with the third song on the album. Better batch a whole pitcher, 'cuz these go down easy.

2 ounces gin

2 ounces fresh grapefruit juice

2 ounces fresh orange juice

1 lime wheel, for garnish

Shake ingredients with ice and pour the drink, ice and all, into a highball glass. Garnish with lime.

SIDE B TANQUERAY NO. TEN "LAID BACK"

Snoop Dogg created this signature drink himself with Tanqueray. It's a tasty treat, *arf arf!*

1 ounce Tanqueray No. TEN

1 ounce Cîroc Apple

2 ounces fresh pineapple juice

2 ounces club soda

Pineapple wedge, for garnish

Shake all ingredients except soda with ice. Strain into a rocks glass filled with ice. Top with soda. Garnish with a pineapple wedge.

Producers: Dr. Dre, Suge Knight   Label: Death Row, Interscope

Buena Vista
Social Club

Social Club
Buena Vista

1997
Genre: Son, Bolero, Danzón, Guajira
When to Spin: Cuban-themed dinner
party

LINER NOTES

In 1996, American guitarist Ry Cooder was in Havana for another project when he began uncovering the music of a long-defunct members-only club that existed from the '40s until the early '60s. Recruiting local musicians, as well as some who had originally played at the club, Cooder recorded this legendary album in just six days (the making of the album was documented by filmmaker Wim Wenders). An international sensation, the release led to a world tour and brought traditional Cuban music to new audiences. The album is infectious, a tour de force of haunting songs that feel like familiar hits even on first listen.

BEFORE YOU DROP THE NEEDLE

Play up the Cuban theme and make some *arroz con pollo* or a big pot of stew, then set out a platter of *tostones* (fried plantains).

SIDE A   DAIQUIRI

Supposedly created by an engineer during the Spanish-American War, this Cuban classic is as easy to make as it is to drink.

> 2 ounces light rum
> 1 ounce fresh lime juice
> ½ ounce simple syrup (page 213)
> Lime wheel, for garnish

Shake ingredients with ice and strain into a chilled cocktail glass. Garnish with lime.

SIDE B   OLD CUBAN

This modern classic by famed New York bartender Audrey Saunders, while not a traditional Cuban drink, has all of the right vibes to accompany this album. Think of it as a love child of the Mojito (page 130) and French 75 (page 118). What isn't better with sparkling wine?

> 1½ ounces aged rum
> 2 dashes of Angostura bitters
> 6 mint leaves
> 1 ounce simple syrup (page 213)
> ¾ ounce fresh lime juice
> 2 ounces sparkling wine
> Mint leaf, for garnish

Muddle mint, syrup, and lime juice in a shaker. Add rum and bitters, then shake with ice. Strain into a coupe glass and top with sparkling wine. Garnish with mint leaf.

IN THE AEROPLANE OVER THE SEA

Neutral Milk Hotel 1998

Genre: Indie Rock   When to Spin: Ugly sweater party

`LINER NOTES` Nothing quite prepares you for your first listen to Jeff Mangum's magnum opus. Urgent, sweeping melodies mix with Eastern European folk and choral music, free jazz, and sound collages to make a kind of folk-y *Sgt. Pepper* of the '90s. A cult album of epic proportions (audiences were singing along at live shows days after its release), it has been touted as a high water mark in contemporary music, with an undeniable emotional pull, as song after song bleeds together to form a perfect, totally engaging experience.

Before you drop the needle:

You know that fugly sweater in the back of your closet? Fish it out. Best-case scenario: by the end of the night you're wearing someone else's. Drinking game: if someone spills a drink, everyone swaps sweaters. If you notice someone has an empty glass, you can demand that they take their sweater off.

SIDE A	SIDE B

PAPER PLANE

Think of this recipe as a riff on the Negroni, replacing sweet vermouth with amaro, Campari with its lighter cousin, Aperol, and gin with bourbon. All that plus a touch of lemon juice to give it some acidity. It is a mighty fine invention by bartender Sam Ross.

¾ ounce bourbon

¾ ounce amaro
(Ross uses Nonino Quintessentia)

¾ ounce Aperol

¾ ounce fresh lemon juice

Shake ingredients with ice and strain into a chilled cocktail glass.

IMPROVED HOLLAND COCKTAIL

"Improved" drinks get their name by receiving additional shine from Maraschino liqueur and/ or absinthe. They appeared first as a group in the back of Jerry Thomas's 1876 cocktail book, *The Bartender's Guide*. Here, the Holland Cocktail gets an upgrade from its original build made with orange curaçao.

2 ounces Genever

½ teaspoon Maraschino liqueur

2 dashes of Angostura bitters

Dash of absinthe

1 teaspoon rich simple syrup
(2:1 sugar to water)

Lemon peel, for garnish

Stir ingredients with ice and strain into a chilled cocktail glass or over a large ice cube in a rocks glass. Garnish with a lemon peel.

LUCINDA WILLIAMS

CAR WHEELS ON A GRAVEL ROAD

1998

LINER NOTES

A legendary album six years in the making, this landmark is a passionate and defiant rockin' country-blues journey, full of love, loss, and regret. It's one of the all-time great Americana albums ever put to wax, and it counts as one of the greatest drinking albums—all grit and dusty back roads. Although considered one of the best songwriters of her generation and a critical darling, the Louisiana-born Williams has never quite achieved commercial success. None of her near-perfect albums have ever charted, including this Grammy Award–winning fifth studio album. Even her hit song, "Passionate Kisses," became a hit for Mary Chapin Carpenter. Channel this primer on southern heartache with drinks served in coffee cups and Mason jars.

BEFORE YOU DROP THE NEEDLE

An ideal album to wake up to or to pop on the turntable when you come home from the bar. Start rolling out some biscuits, or whip up some eggs and grits.

SIDE A BOURBON AND COFFEE

The title track calls forth breakfast at a kitchen table with coffee, eggs, and bacon. Grab the closest mug and don't get fussy.

2 ounces bourbon
1 cup hot coffee
Splash of half-and-half
Demerara sugar or maple syrup, to taste

Combine ingredients in a hot mug and stir.

SIDE B TENNESSEE MANHATTAN

This drink is a nod to Nashville, where this album was recorded. A Manhattan it is not, but that's the idea, right? We like to serve it in a Mason jar. Whiskey and cherry love each other (as Manhattan drinkers know), and using cherry syrup is a quick and dirty substitute for sweet vermouth, making this a cheap, no-fuss thirst-quencher.

2 ounces Tennessee whiskey
Dash of Angostura bitters
1 Maraschino cherry, with a little syrup
2 to 3 ounces club soda

Stir whiskey, Angostura, and cherry syrup with ice in a rocks glass. Top with club soda and garnish.

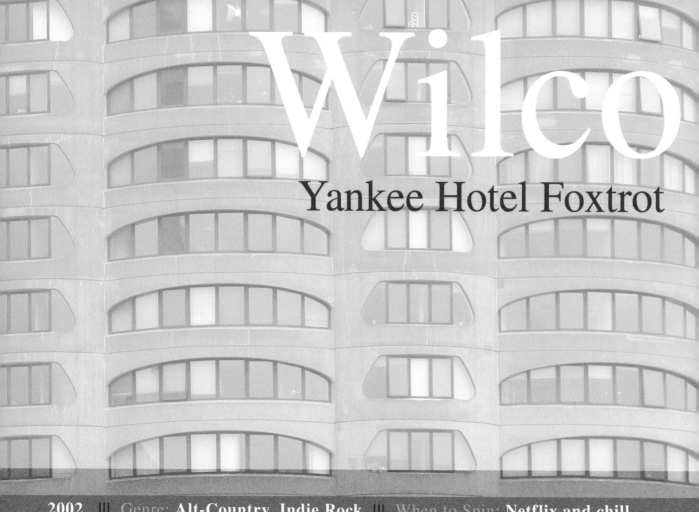

Wilco

Yankee Hotel Foxtrot

2002 ||| Genre: **Alt-Country, Indie Rock** ||| When to Spin: **Netflix and chill**

LINER NOTES   *Yankee Hotel Foxtrot* suffered a legendarily difficult gestation before being trumpeted at release as one of the great—if not *the greatest*—album of the new millennium. First, the band left Reprise because the label considered the record a career-ender. Then, the album was slated to be released on September 11, 2001—but the label snafu miraculously delayed it until April of 2002. For fans who had grown up with the band, YHF was the culmination of a decades-long conversation. *Wilco* had brought impeccably crafted, intelligent alt-country rock to the fore from their native Chicago, and this album felt like a summation.

BEFORE YOU DROP THE NEEDLE   Take inspo from the image on the album cover and assemble some Chicago-style hot dogs.

SIDE A: FISHBOWL

YHF opens with Jeff Tweedy crooning the line, "I am an American aquarium drinker."
Now, when the first lyrics are the singer confessing he can drink as much as an
aquarium can hold, you know you're listening to a great drinking album. The song
plunges the listener back into the lost dreams of youth. And we go along, pairing this
deeply nostalgic album with a classic collegiate fishbowl. You'll want to judge it. You'll
want to think you're above it. And that is the point—where'd your innocence go? Be
sure to pick up some colorful eighteen-inch straws, plenty of garnish, and drop in some
Swedish Fish.

Serves 2 to 4

5 ounces vodka

5 ounces light rum

2½ ounces blue curaçao liqueur

2½ ounces fresh lemon juice

2½ ounces coconut cream (Coco
   Lopez)

8 ounces fresh pineapple juice

8 ounces ginger beer or lemon-lime
   soda

For garnish: skewered citrus moons,
   cherries, pineapple, edible orchids

Mix ingredients in a pitcher. When
you're ready to dive in, fill a fishbowl
with ice. Transfer mixture from the
pitcher and garnish lavishly. Add
straws and slurp.

Note: we like to use a whole fresh
pineapple for this recipe. We'll
juice half of it, then use the rest for
garnish, including a few of the spiked
leaves.

SIDE A: BOURBON (IN A DIXIE CUP)

There is a lot of bourbon in Wilco songs, from the opening track which references "disposable Dixie cup drinking" to the track "Poor Places," where Tweedy sings, "There's bourbon on the breath / Of the singer you love so much / He takes all his words from the books / That you don't read anyway." What a jerk.

1½ ounces bourbon

Pour bourbon into a Dixie cup. Serve.

BONUS TRACK

Play this indie listen as you mix up some drinks, then sit back and watch the documentary about the making of the album, *I Am Trying to Break Your Heart*.

Producer: Wilco   Label: Nonesuc

Turn on the Bright Lights

INTERPOL

LINER NOTES

Dark, romantic, and claustrophobic, Interpol's debut album captured the desiccated emotional landscape of the country following 9/11. The record rose out of the extraordinarily vibrant NYC music scene of the early 2000s to capture a haunting mood with energy and chemistry. While comparisons to Joy Division are inevitable, the album is something new: spare and brooding with enough forward momentum to deliver insistent rock 'n' roll.

BEFORE YOU DROP THE NEEDLE

Turn off all the lights. Glow-in-the-dark face paint is encouraged. Or, pass out glow-in-the-dark stars and use this as an occasion to reimagine the universe in your living room.

2002 ||| Genre: Indie Rock, Post-Punk Revival ||| When to Spin: Glow-in-the-dark party

SIDE A   BLACK MANHATTAN

Created by Todd Smith when he was at San Francisco's Bourbon & Branch, this riff on the classic calls for replacing sweet vermouth with amaro. The result is your new favorite drink.

- 2 ounces rye whiskey
- 1 ounce amaro (Smith uses Averna)
- Dash of orange bitters
- Dash of Angostura bitters
- Cherry, for garnish

Stir ingredients with ice and strain into a chilled cocktail glass. Garnish with a cherry.

SIDE B   INTERPOL

Created by bartender Kyle Davidson at Blackbird in Chicago, this drink employs Cardamaro, a wine-based amaro traditionally consumed as a digestif. One would think that with a name like Cardamaro, the chief ingredient would be cardamom—but it's infused with cardoon, a vegetable that tastes reminiscent of artichoke. This vegetal amaro makes for great cocktails when in masterful hands, as it is in this drink.

- 1 ounce Citadelle gin
- 1½ ounces Cardamaro
- ½ ounce lemon juice

Shake ingredients with ice and strain into a cocktail glass.

Producers: Gareth Jones, Peter Katis   Label: Matador

BACK TO BLACK

AMY WINEHOUSE

2006 Genre: Soul, R&B, Neo Soul   When to Spin: Chill-out grill-out

LINER NOTES

The second studio album for power-house vocalist Amy Winehouse, *Back to Black* finds her sifting through the sounds of girl groups from the 1950s and '60s, like the Supremes and the Shangri-las. From this inspiration, she created a retro album with a modern sensibility—a soul classic. Winehouse's fearless, brassy voice delivers the punch here, capturing heartache with a raw honesty that is both compelling and beautiful.

BEFORE YOU DROP THE NEEDLE

This is one of our favorite albums to play at an outdoor dinner party (baby back ribs, wine glasses in hand). Skip the fancy sides, and keep the grill going all night.

A

CALIMOCHO (OR KALIMOTXO)

The Calimocho is simplicity itself: inexpensive red wine and cola. It's an unfussy combination from Spain that is similar to a mimosa or a spritzer. We prefer using soda with cane sugar for added flavor, so hunt down Mexican Coke if you can. The result tastes like cherry cola—use a jammy red wine (such as Grenache or Shiraz). For a variation, try lemon-lime soda.

3 ounces red wine

3 ounces cola

Lime wedge, for garnish

Combine wine and cola in cups filled with ice. Garnish with a lime wedge.

B

ABSINTHE FRAPPÉ

Want to keep this party going? Break out the bottle of absinthe and get in tune with Winehouse's haunting restlessness on Side B. Less fussy than traditional absinthe service (forget the spoon and the sugar cube), the Absinthe Frappé is wildly refreshing. To make crushed ice, just fill a resealable bag with ice cubes and break out a tenderizer or rolling pin.

1½ ounces absinthe

½ ounce simple syrup (page 213)

2 ounces club soda

Mint sprig, for garnish

Shake absinthe and simple syrup, then strain over a small rocks glass heaped with crushed ice. Garnish with mint, and serve with a straw.

Producers: Mark Ronson, Salaam Remi

Label: Island

VAMPIRE WEEKEND

LINER NOTES Vampire Weekend's debut album is an unabashedly preppy and quirky mix of yacht rock and Afro-beat. With videos shot on boats and nerdy lyrics referencing classical architecture, the smart-ass whimsy of these Ivy Leaguers set college radio ablaze, creating legions of hipster fans. The songs "Mansard Roof" and "Campus" are sure to charm your argyle socks off.

BEFORE YOU DROP THE NEEDLE Slip into your boat shoes and preppy shirt, then make like you're at the marina. If you're feeling festive, serve some Shrimp Lettuce Wraps (page 163).

2008   **GENRE:** Indie Rock, Indie Pop, World Beat   **WHEN TO SPIN:** Yacht rock party

SIDE A OXFORD COMMA

This recipe from bartender Jeremy Oertel combines herbaceous Chartreuse and celery flavors for a fresh drink that boasts just a touch of sweetness from the cherry liqueur. While the combo may sound a little strange and vegetal, it just might be your new favorite. Oertel claims the cocktail wasn't specifically named for the second song on this album, but does that matter? It's a match. Note: Bittermens Celery Shrub is available online. Use a hefty dropperful of it, and this cocktail really comes together.

2 ounces gin (Oertel calls for Plymouth)
¾ ounce dry vermouth
½ ounce green Chartreuse
1 teaspoon Maraschino liqueur
Dash of Bittermens Celery Shrub
Lemon peel, for garnish

Stir ingredients with ice and strain into a chilled cocktail glass. Garnish with a lemon peel.

SIDE B CAPE COD COOLER

Ah yes, the preppy drink of choice. You can almost taste the Izod shirt and the Sperry Top-Siders. Part of a flotilla of drinks featuring cranberry juice (Sea Breeze, Bay Breeze, Madras, Woo Woo), the Cape Codder came to prominence in the '60s, when Ocean Spray pushed cranberry juice to the masses. It doesn't hurt that this is a mighty tasty quencher that's a cinch to mix. "Kwassa Kwassa," bitches.

2 ounces vodka
2½ ounces cranberry juice
½ ounce fresh lime juice
1 to 2 ounces club soda
Lime slice, for garnish

Shake all ingredients, except the club soda, with ice and strain into an ice-filled collins glass. Top with club soda and garnish with a slice of lime.

MUNCHIES! :: SHRIMP LETTUCE WRAPS

We like to Old Bay out our shrimp salad and serve it on lettuce boats at parties. A whole tray of these looks especially nice if you garnish them with a few extra chopped scallions and sliced radishes.

Combine yogurt, vinegar, lemon juice, hot sauce, Worcestershire sauce, and Old Bay in a medium bowl. Add shrimp, celery, cucumber, scallions, and radishes and stir to coat. Season with salt and pepper to taste. Cover and chill in the refrigerator until ready to serve. Serve in lettuce leaves.

Serves 4 to 6

½ cup low-fat yogurt
1 teaspoon white wine vinegar
1½ teaspoons fresh lemon juice
Dash of hot sauce
¼ teaspoon Worcestershire sauce
1 teaspoon Old Bay Seasoning
1 pound cooked shrimp, peeled and deveined
½ cup finely chopped celery
¼ cup finely diced English cucumber
¼ cup thinly sliced scallions
4 radishes, finely diced
Sea salt and black pepper, to taste
Head of romaine lettuce,
   or 2 heads of Bibb lettuce

seduce

"If music be the food of love, play on."   —William Shakespeare, *Twelfth Night*

FRANK SINATRA x MILES DAVIS o THE BEACH BOYS x THE DOORS
LEONARD COHEN o ISAAC HAYES x NEIL YOUNG o JONI MITCHELL x MARVIN GAYE
AL GREEN o STEVIE WONDER x THE SMITHS o THE CURE x RADIOHEAD o BON IVER

Part of vinyl's appeal is the way it feels in your hands—removing a platter from its sleeve, pressing it down on a turntable, sliding the needle into a groove. There's visual attraction, too, if there's a wild cover or an intriguing list of song titles. As any collector will tell you, vinyl is sensual.

The albums in this chapter are especially seductive. Joni Mitchell sings about her fishnet stockings, Leonard Cohen croons to Suzanne, Marianne, and a "Winter Lady." It's impossible not to feel amorous while listening through this list. Granted, it can be a drag to flip a record during a make-out session, but think about it: What's more romantic than settling in to listen to records together? Netflix and chill, or vinyl and . . .?

Candy is dandy, but cocktails are quicker. Learn how to woo with a classic Manhattan (page 170), a wild Whizz Bang (page 203), or a lovely Bosom Caresser (page 183). The drinks in this section are time-honored concoctions of seduction.

In the Wee Small Hours

Frank

Liner Notes

Sinatra's career reached a low point in the early 1950s, rebounding some with his appearance in the film *From Here to Eternity* in 1953, plus a couple of successful records. And his personal life was a disaster—he left his wife for actress Ava Gardner in 1951, then Gardner left him shortly thereafter. This album channels his lovesick blues, with the singer's voice conveying great emotion through songs of loss, depression, and loneliness. Regarded as a "concept album," it was recorded entirely at night, with anecdotal accounts of Sinatra breaking down and crying during the takes. Despite the pain, he remained meticulous throughout and produced what is considered to be his masterpiece.

Before You Drop the Needle

Plan a dress-up date, and pop this on the hi-fi before you head off to dinner. Of course, it also works after dinner. Fix a couple drinks, and prepare to dance cheek to cheek.

Sinatra

1955

A ~ B

Manhattan

What's to be said about the Manhattan cocktail? The first and finest marriage of grain and grape, the unaccompanied Bach of drinks, the one cocktail to rule them all! Sip it with Sinatra and you get a sublime sense of time and place. Over the ages, so many lips have tasted the classic's charm. Lean into the glass and a Manhattan always whispers, "You are not alone."

2 ounces rye whiskey

1 ounce sweet vermouth

2 dashes of Angostura bitters

Cherry, for garnish

Stir ingredients with ice and strain into a cocktail glass. Garnish with a cherry.

Tuxedo Cocktail

A variation on the Martini (page 33), this classic swaps sherry for vermouth, gaining a pleasantly nutty flavor. The drink gets its name from the ritzy planned community once in Tuxedo Park, outside of Jersey City. In 1886, a few of the town's men chopped the tails off of their suits and the "Tuxedo" was born. The drink hailing from Tuxedo Park became a staple at the Waldorf Astoria bar, which catered to "Tuxedo-ites."

2 ounces gin

1 ounce fino sherry

Dash of orange bitters

Lemon peel, for garnish

Stir ingredients with ice and strain into a chilled cocktail glass. Garnish with lemon peel.

Producer: Voyle Gilmore   Label: Capitol

MILES
KIND OF BLUE

LINER NOTES

A contemplative masterpiece, the best-selling and most influential jazz record of all time is ambient, melancholic, and romantic. Once you hear it, it's unforgettable. At the time of its release, *Kind of Blue* offered an entirely new sound, based on improvising beyond structured chord changes. It showed a way forward from Davis's prior bebop sound into uncharted territory. Recorded in just a few takes over two days in New York, the album is a poignant moment of recording perfection. A musical journey of great beauty and sensitivity, and one that can be played often as the background to a cultured life.

STEREO
CS 8163

COLUMBIA

DAVIS

A BUMBLE BEE

Frothy and approachable, this drink is sure to woo any prospective jazzer or jazette. A classic from Charles H. Baker's travels recorded in *The South American Gentleman's Companion* (worth a read), it is plush with just a slight sting. Relax into its soft embrace.

    2 ounces dark rum
    ¾ ounce fresh lime juice
    1 ounce honey syrup
       (1:1 honey to water)
    ½ ounce egg white

Shake ingredients vigorously with ice and strain into a cocktail glass.

B MARTINEZ

This album has always been employed to impress a certain sophistication. And nothing says you know what's up like a little extra cocktail history. Behold the Martinez! Really more a style of drink than a cocktail, it is the combination from which the Martini springs. Think of it as a bridge between the modern Martini and its elder sibling, the Manhattan. Likely first made with the old Dutch style gin, Genever, nowadays it often contains Old Tom gin (a sweeter style). This cocktail is refined and nuanced. If you know it and drink it, it is says you are an erudite and urbane member of the cocktail club—and thus obviously good in the sack.

    2 ounces Old Tom gin
    1 ounce sweet vermouth
    1 teaspoon Maraschino liqueur
    2 dashes of orange bitters
    Lemon twist, for garnish

Stir ingredients with ice and strain into a chilled cocktail glass. Garnish with a lemon twist.

Producers: Teo Macero, Irving Townsend   Label: Columbia

The Beach Boys

Pet Sounds

Genre:
Rock, Pop, Psychedelic Rock

When to Spin:
Heavy petting . . . 'cuz "Pet Sounds"!

1966

LINER NOTES

Pet Sounds offers a full atmospheric experience, a world of sun-worship and wonder that is deeply romantic. Written by Brian Wilson, who consciously set out to make the greatest rock album ever, the record signaled a watershed change in pop music from danceable pop and rock to serious listening recordings. It's hard to imagine that this lush album, full of vocal harmonies and sound effects, wasn't a huge hit when it was first released. Songs like "Hang on to Your Ego" and "Wouldn't It Be Nice" are now classics, conjuring the boardwalk innocence of young summer lovers. Break out your cutoffs and flip-flops.

BEFORE YOU DROP THE NEEDLE

Cultivate some California vibes with a beach blanket and some coconut lotion. To go all-out, flank your bed with potted palms and serve your lover these drinks with tiny paper umbrellas.

SIDE A PIÑA COLADA

Dreamy and luscious, this drink has been lubricating the path to the bedroom since at least the early 1960s. Even if it is a bit silly, the voluptuous charms of a Piña Colada are undeniable—all pleasing flavor and texture. Drinking one says you are optimistic and willing to be frivolous. If you want to toss in a pro move here, add a pinch of sea salt to offset the sweetness.

2½ ounces light rum
Dash of Angostura bitters
3 ounces fresh pineapple juice
1 ounce coconut cream (Coco Lopez)
Pineapple wedge, for garnish

Blend ingredients with about 1 cup of ice and serve in a chilled collins or hurricane glass. Garnish with a pineapple wedge.

SIDE B WATERMELON COOLER

Sunset in a glass? Yes, kick back with your babe and make out like you're on the beach.

2 ounces light rum
½ ounce Cointreau
½ ounce fresh lime juice
½ ounce simple syrup (page 213)
1 cup watermelon, seeded and chopped
Lime wheel, for garnish

Blend ingredients with about 1 cup of ice. Taste and add more lime or more simple syrup, if necessary. Pour into a chilled rocks glass or wine glass. Garnish with a lime wheel.

THE DOORS

1967 • **Genre:** Rock, Psychedelic Rock • **When to Spin:** Psychedelic sleep-over

LINER NOTES The Doors were named after the Aldous Huxley book *Doors of Perception*, in turn a line from a William Blake poem. Heady and dark stuff for a fresh rock 'n' roll band from sunny L.A. The group's debut album features a lead singer who looked like a Greek god crooning over a guitar, and contains many of the band's best -known songs: "Light My Fire," "Break on Through (to the Other Side)," and "The End." Poetic, lugubrious, yet hard-rocking, the album captures the primal feel of the group's live performances and stands as a complete album, not just as a collection of songs. A psychedelic masterpiece in a minor key, it feels stoned while remaining clean and smartly trippy. **BEFORE YOU DROP THE NEEDLE** Drape a scarf over your lampshade or plug in the lava lamp to set the mood. This is a great pillows-on-the-floor kind of listen.

SIDE A

WHISKEY DAISY

Oye, take us to ze next viskey bah! This is the drink to sip while listening to the Doors cover Bertolt Brecht's drinking song from *The Three Penny Opera*, "Alabama Song." Whiskey Daisy recipes are all over the map. Some call for triple sec or Grand Marnier, while others call for grenadine. Many dispense with the soda in early recipes, and end up with a sort of sour. Or a fizz. Or who-knows-what. We make our own franken-daisy thusly.

2 ounces whiskey
1 ounce fresh lemon juice
1 ounce Cointreau
½ teaspoon simple syrup (page 213)
1 ounce club soda
Slice of orange, for garnish
Sprig of mint, for garnish (optional)

Shake ingredients, except soda, with ice and strain into a chilled collins glass filled with crushed ice. Top with soda. Garnish with an orange slice and a sprig of mint (if you like).

SIDE B

BIJOU

Bijou is French for "jewel," and the drink is so named because of its lustrous color. Properly, it's made with red sweet vermouth, but we like to use bianco vermouth (a sweet white vermouth) to achieve a stunning green color. While this isn't exactly "correct," we think it's an improvement. Morrison's connection to French poetry is the stuff of legend. He's even buried in Père Lachaise Cemetery in Paris. We honor him with perhaps the most stunning of classic French cocktails.

1½ ounces gin
¾ ounce green Chartreuse
1 ounce bianco vermouth
2 dashes of orange bitters

Stir ingredients with ice and strain into a chilled cocktail glass.

elektra

Producer: Paul A. Rothchild   Label: Elektra

Songs of
Leonard Cohen

1967

Genre:
Folk, Folk Rock

When to Spin:
Cabin weekend

LINER NOTES

Mystical and deeply melodic, these songs make for some seriously soothing drinking music. Cohen was both a poet and something of a foodie, so listen closely and you'll hear mentions of bread, wine, honey, tea, and oranges. It's comfort music. Pack your record player in the trunk of your car, grab the cat and dog, then head to the woods with a longtime love or a new infatuation. With its many references to winter ("Winter Lady") and shivering Eskimos, this may just be the sleeper holiday album you've been looking for—slightly melancholic but sumptuously cozy.

BEFORE YOU DROP THE NEEDLE

Pull out the wool blanket and light the woodstove. Or pretend with a pine-scented candle.

BLOOD AND SAND

One of the greatest Scotch-based cocktails, this classic drink was named after the eponymous 1922 movie starring Rudolph Valentino as a bullfighter. With Cherry Heering starring as the "blood," it is a knock-your-red-cape-off combination that is more than the sum of its parts. Even non-Scotch drinkers love it (just don't tell them it's Scotch until they've tried it). Cohen is all sex, death, and gravitas—and this is the drink to match it.

1½ ounces Scotch (we like Talisker)
¾ ounce Cherry Heering
¾ ounce sweet vermouth
1 ounce fresh orange juice
Orange peel, for garnish

Shake ingredients with ice and strain into a chilled cocktail glass. Garnish with an orange peel.

WHITE LADY

Cohen loved the ladies, and his songs are populated with nuns, saints, and lovers. Pour a frothy one and toast "Sisters of Mercy." You'll want this one as a last sip when Cohen starts whistling and straining to finish his "la-las" on the last song.

1½ ounces gin
¾ ounce Cointreau
¾ ounce fresh lemon juice
½ ounce rich simple syrup (2:1 sugar and water)
1 ounce egg white
Lemon twist, for garnish

Shake ingredients vigorously with ice and strain into a chilled cocktail glass. Garnish with a lemon twist.

Producer: John Simon   Label: Columbia

MUNCHIES!

Channel the good feels here. This mellow soup was inspired by Cohen's mention of tea, wine, and oranges—hence the orange zest and a splash of red wine at the end. We kept the ingredient list simple to make packing easy for a weekend away. Pair it with a hunk of rustic cheese, a loaf of bread, and a jug of red wine.

Serves 4

2 strips bacon (or pancetta),
  roughly chopped
1 medium onion, chopped
1 celery stalk, chopped
3 cloves garlic, minced
½ teaspoon dried thyme
1 teaspoon smoked paprika
1 quart chicken stock
1 bay leaf
1 large sweet potato,
  peeled and diced
2 roma tomatoes, chopped
1 can (15-ounce) chickpeas, drained
1½ cups spinach leaves, packed
2 tablespoons red wine
Sea salt, to taste
Fresh orange zest, to garnish

Heat bacon in a medium stockpot over high heat until it begins to brown, about 3 minutes, then lower the heat to medium and add onion and celery. Sauté until it begins to soften, about 3 minutes, then add garlic, thyme, and paprika. Cook, stirring occasionally for another 3 to 4 minutes. Add chicken stock, bay leaf, sweet potato, tomatoes, and chickpeas, then bring to a boil. Lower the heat and simmer for 15 minutes, or until potatoes are fork-tender. Add spinach and wine a few minutes before serving, along with salt. Garnish with orange zest.

Hot Buttered Soul
ISAAC HAYES

1969   Genre: **Soul, Funk, R&B**   When to Spin: **DIY spa night**

Producers: Al Bell, Marvell Thomas, Allen Jones   Label: Enterprise

LINER NOTES

This is a sprawling, landmark soul album that became a reality only after Stax records split with Atlantic. Hayes's first album didn't sell well, and he was prepared to return to producing, when Stax head Al Bell suddenly granted Hayes complete creative control over a new recording. Thickly sweet strings, sweeping R&B guitar, jazz drums, and Hayes's velvety voice give this album its opulence. The whole thing feels luxurious and excessive, and it's the perfect album for extending that feeling into a party or romantic evening.

BEFORE YOU DROP THE NEEDLE

Go full-on with face masks, scented lotion, fluffy robes, and white candles. Don't forget cucumber slices for your eyes and, if you want to go the extra mile, a foot bath.

SIDE A HOT BUTTERED RUM

Sweet, warm, creamy, and comforting, this is a classic drink that we now consume only during cold months. Originally, though, it was enjoyed year-round. You forget just how sexy it is, all those exotic flavors and a luscious buttery texture. It sure beats tea.

2 ounces dark rum
1 small slice soft butter
1 teaspoon brown sugar
Optional spices, to taste: cinnamon, nutmeg, allspice, cloves
4 to 6 ounces hot water

In the bottom of a warm mug, combine butter, brown sugar, and spices. Add rum, vanilla, and hot water. Stir.

SIDE B BOSOM CARESSER

This drink appears in *The Savoy Cocktail* Book and has become a classic for the name alone. Good thing its orange-y flavor is a delight. Just note there is curaçao, *and then there is curaçao.* If you use a cheap version in a plastic bottle from the bottom shelf of the liquor store, you'll taste it. We highly recommend Pierre Ferrand dry curaçao, and we're not paid to say it. Also, fear not the egg yolk. It makes the cocktail soft and *plushhhhhh.*

1½ ounces brandy
¾ ounce orange curaçao
1 teaspoon grenadine (page 212)
1 egg yolk

Shake ingredients vigorously with ice and strain into a chilled cocktail glass.

AFTER THE GOLD RUSH   NEIL YOUNG

1970   Genre: Rock, Country, Folk   When to Spin: You're making him/her dinner during sweater weather

LINER NOTES: Inspired by and named after a Dean Stockwell screenplay, Young's album was released following the sensation of *Déjà Vu* with Crosby, Stills, Nash & Young. While critical reception was cool, with many feeling the album was rushed to production, it endures as perhaps Young's masterpiece—the very sloppiness of it making it feel honest, personal, and compelling. The album is an emotional roller coaster, with songs ranging from hippie hymns to the hard-rocking "Southern Man." Young's whining voice and electric guitar lead us through love, loss, and introspection for a hopeful—if heart-wrenching—thing of beauty.

BEFORE YOU DROP THE NEEDLE Pick up around the house, grab some groceries, and light a few candles. You've got this.

SIDE A: GOLD RUSH

Balanced and delicious, this is one cocktail to always keep in the quiver—it's a real pleaser and goes down easy. Created by T. J. Siegal at the original Milk & Honey bar in New York, it has become a modern classic.

2 ounces bourbon
¾ ounce fresh lemon juice
¾ ounce honey syrup (1:1 honey to water)

Shake ingredients with ice and strain into a rocks glass filled with ice.

SIDE B: CAMPFIRE SLING

So it's a little funny that this cocktail hails from Los Angeles, given that it's full of cool-weather flavors. But this combination by Kevin Felker at Water Grill is a simple, foolproof drink that will get you cozy fast. Plus, the flamed peel is sure to impress (see instructions for Flame of Love, page 81).

2 ounces rye whiskey
3 dashes of chocolate bitters
¼ ounce maple syrup
Orange peel, for garnish

Combine ingredients in a rocks glass with ice and stir. Flame an orange peel over the drink.

Producers: Neil Young, David Briggs, Kendall Pacios   Label: Reprise

BLUE

JONI MITCHELL

1971

genre:

Folk, Folk Rock

when to spin:

Karmic cleanse

liner notes

With a title like *Blue*, you might think this album is all rainy-day feels, but despite some melancholy, the songs feel drenched in sun. Like an alto kitty-cat, Joni Mitchell purred her way through the '70s and set the tone for a decade of wine-drunk afternoons spent listening to her wistful lyrics about loving the wrong man (try drinking each time you hear the word "daddy" or an allusion to an old lover). Here's what we love about a deep listen: each song on this critically acclaimed album feels like a different-colored room full of Mitchell's personal belongings. Old letters, flowers, poems, hand-knit sweaters, French cologne—they're strewn throughout these lyrics, creating an intimate portrait of pining. Play Blue when you're feeling hopelessly romantic.

before you drop the needle:

This album is best enjoyed while sitting cross-legged on the floor surrounded by burning incense. Plan a trip with someone, share big dreams, build vision boards.

SIDE A

santorini sunrise

Mitchell's song "Carey" was written on the island of Crete, where she lived for a time with a cave-dwelling hippie community in 1970. The recording features Stephen Stills on bass and acoustic guitar, and Mitchell's mad dulcimer skills. Hum along as you sip on this cocktail developed at the Greek seafood restaurant, Molyvos, in NYC. Despite the strange combination of ingredients, this drink is so refreshing and delicious. Note: a splash of club soda is a lovely addition here.

2 ounces ouzo

1 ounce Campari

3 ounces fresh pink grapefruit juice

2 teaspoons honey

2 wheels pink grapefruit, quartered (8 total pieces), divided

4 mint leaves, plus a sprig for garnish

Muddle all but one of the grapefruit slices together with mint leaves and honey in a collins glass. Fill with ice and add liquids. Stir. Garnish with the remaining grapefruit slice and a mint sprig.

SIDE B

mixed berry sangria

Wine and bright colors infuse this album, making a transcendent sangria essential. To add to a beautiful presentation here, freeze a few berries and mint leaves in ice cube trays, then drop the ice into a pitcher of this sangria just before serving.

Serves 4 to 6

½ cup Cherry Heering

1 bottle (750 ml) light red wine, like Beaujolais or Pinot Noir

¼ cup honey

2 ounces lemon juice

1 cup blueberries

1 cup raspberries

1 cup blackberries

Club soda, to taste

In a pitcher, combine honey and Cherry Heering. Add the wine, lemon juice, berries, and stir. Top with club soda. Serve over ice.

Producer: Joni Mitchell   Label: Reprise

WHAT'S GOING ON

MARVIN GAYE

1973

GENRE: MOTOWN, FUNK, SMOOTH SOUL

WHEN TO SPIN: BREAKFAST IN BED

LINER NOTES

Beloved for his milky voice and carnal energy, Marvin Gaye is to Motown what orange juice is to breakfast. He's essential listening for anyone looking to run some sweet charm on a new infatuation or repair a strained romantic situation. It's impossible to feel sad or panicked with Marvin on the turntable—no wonder this album was a best seller for two years after it was released. Bizarre fact: the title track was originally written as a gospel song, then turned into a protest song. Today, it's still one of the sexiest sets of slow beats you can find on vinyl.

BEFORE YOU DROP THE NEEDLE

Fix some drinks and bring them into the boudoir.

'Nuff said.

SIDE A

SOUL KISS NO. 2

This is a vintage cocktail from the 1930s that existed long before Soul became a musical movement, but its smooth mix of Canadian Club Whisky and fresh OJ seems like an appropriate entrée into a dreamy morning or evening listening party. Dubonnet, a ruby-colored aperitif from France, gives this drink body and color. Oh, yeahhh.

2 ounces Canadian Club Whisky

¼ ounce dry vermouth

¼ ounce Dubonnet

½ ounce freshly squeezed orange juice

Slice of orange, to garnish

Shake ingredients with ice and strain into a chilled cocktail glass. Float half an orange wheel on top.

SIDE B

VELVET HAMMER

On Sunday mornings, we love to listen to *What's Goin' On*, and the Velvet Hammer makes a perfect pairing for two reasons: 1) listen to the lyrics and you'll notice that for all his sweet crooning, Gaye's lyrics deliver a serious and powerful message, and 2) this drink is beyond amazing served with French toast or doughnuts.

1 ounce Cointreau

1 ounce coffee liqueur

1 ounce half-and-half

Shake ingredients with ice and strain over ice into a chilled rocks glass.

Producer: Marvin Gaye   Label: Tamala/Motown

AVOCADO MANGO TOASTS

Sweet and a little spicy, these toasts are exactly what you want to eat in bed, and they're much easier to fix than fried eggs and bacon. Try serving them in the morning with a Soul Kiss No. 2 (page 190) and keep that record going!

SERVES 2

2 ripe avocados

Half a lime

½ teaspoon sea salt

2 slices of bread, toasted

1 ripe mango, peeled and sliced

Smoked paprika or chile flakes

Slice avocado and toss with lime juice and sea salt. Arrange on toasts with slices of mango. Sprinkle with paprika or chile flakes.

GREATEST HITS

Al Green

1975 Genre: Soul When to Spin: Date with your soul mate

LINER NOTES

Behold the auditory Xanax that is Al Green. This album was released as a collection of most of Green's hits in 1975, and has had a life of its own, introducing generations to this smooth soul singer with a mind-blowing falsetto. The recording oozes with yearning and sexuality, all sweet strings and calm organ music. It is perfect for a chill gathering, or as a cue that it's time to slow dance and make love.

Prepare to trade massages, cook dinner together,
or set aside time to stare into each other's eyes.

SIDE A
HANKY PANKY

A classic cocktail credited to the famed drinkstress Ada "Coley" Coleman at the Savoy Hotel in London, the Hanky Panky is sometimes called the Fernet-Branca Cocktail. While the name has sexual overtones today, back in the day it just meant "black magic." Coleman created this for actor Charles Hawtrey, and while we don't know exactly what they had going on, this voluptuous drink says it all.

1½ ounces London dry gin
1½ ounces sweet vermouth
¼ ounce Fernet-Branca
Orange twist, for garnish

Stir ingredients with ice and strain into a chilled cocktail glass. Garnish with an orange twist.

SIDE B
ARCHANGEL

Religious overtones abound in this album, and we adore this cocktail. Somehow it screams Al Green, and we pair the two every time. Credited to Michael McIlroy and Richard Boccato of the famed bar Milk & Honey in New York, it is a modern classic. Try this with Hendricks gin if you want to emphasize the cucumber. Otherwise, we like to use Plymouth or Beefeater.

2¼ ounces gin
¾ ounce Aperol
2 slices cucumber
   (cut to a half-inch thickness)
Lemon twist, for garnish

Muddle cucumber in the bottom of a mixing glass. Add gin, Aperol, and ice. Stir. Strain into a chilled cocktail glass and garnish with a lemon twist. Note: you may want to double-strain this drink if you use cucumbers with seeds.

Producer: Willie Mitchell   Label: Motown

MOTOWN

SONGS IN THE KEY OF LIFE

STEVIE WONDER

19
76

GENRE: SOUL, JAZZ, FUNK, R&B

WHEN TO SPIN: MARATHON MAKE-OUT SESSION

LINER NOTES Lengthy and sprawling, this double album is a true listening experience. Amazingly, *Songs in the Key of Life* was Stevie Wonder's eighteenth studio album. It became the best-selling and most acclaimed recording of his career, and one of the most important ever made. Think of the record as an awe-inspiring tour through a variety of musical styles and emotional landscapes, from mellow to ecstatic to deeply moving. It is a peak artistic statement. **BEFORE YOU DROP THE NEEDLE** Power through this exquisite double album by making an extra-large batch of drinks. They're healthy, right? This is a great post-workout listen, deeply relaxing but also energizing.

SIDE A GREEN JUICE COCKTAIL

Although it's tempting to pair this album with a frothy egg cocktail, we honor Stevie Wonder's vegan lifestyle here with an enervating drink to fuel you through a long listen (twenty-one songs in all). Get out your juicer and serve this up while donning a dashiki tunic, Wonder's fashion statement of choice.

Serves 2 ||| 4 ounces gin or tequila | 2 cups spinach | 2 cups peeled and diced cucumber | 2 celery stalks | ½ teaspoon grated gingerroot | 3 sprigs parsley | 2 green apples, peeled, cored, and diced | Juice of 1 lemon

Juice ingredients, except for the gin or tequila, together. Pour 2 ounces gin or tequila into two rocks glasses and top with blended juice.

SIDE B SPRING FEELING

This is our go-to Chartreuse cocktail when we want something on the dry side. The recipe is so incredibly simple and fantastic that we are loathe to leave it out of the vinyl lover's arsenal. We adapt it here from *The Savoy Cocktail Book* of 1930. It's bright, fresh, and enlivening, just like the lyrics of this album.

2 ounces gin | 1 ounce green Chartreuse | 1 ounce lemon juice

Shake ingredients with ice and strain into a chilled cocktail glass.

THE
QUEEN
IS
DEAD

Genre: Alternative Rock, Post-Punk, Indie Rock   **When to Spin:** Crosswords in bed

The Smiths

LINER NOTES

By turns petulant and gregarious, erudite and downright silly, the third studio album by the Smiths is a jangly pop landscape listeners enter by way of Morrissey's captivating lyrics. It is a contemplative record worth repeat listens, and features the band's single, "Bigmouth Strikes Again," but also the great ode to camaraderie, "There Is a Light That Never Goes Out." Highly regarded, critics at the British mag *NME* have named this the greatest album of all time, besting the Beatles and the Stones. High praise, but as the sheer audacity and intelligence become clear, they're not necessarily wrong. Give your love a bouquet of lilacs, hold hands, and nestle in for a listen.

EFORE YOU DROP THE NEEDLE

rab the dictionary and your mixing glass. Nothing else is needed.

A

Royal Pimm's Cup

We like our "regular" Pimm's cups with ginger ale, but here we fancy the drink up a bit for the Mozzer with Champagne. Created by the owner of an oyster bar, Pimm's is a mixture of herbs and liqueurs in a gin base. It's well balanced on its own, so it doesn't require a lot of doctoring to display its charms in a cocktail. Pimm's Cups are beautiful both to drink and to behold.

2 ounces Pimm's #1

1 cucumber slice

1 orange slice

1 strawberry, sliced

3 ounces Champagne or other sparkling wine

Sprig of mint, for garnish

Combine Pimm's, cucumber, and fruit in a collins glass. Muddle. Top with ice and Champagne. Garnish with a sprig of mint.

B

Obituary

The queen is dead. Long live the queen. A classic New Orleans cocktail that upgrades a gin Martini with the green fairy, this drink will surely wake the dead. The botanicals of the absinthe combine here with gin's bracing cleanness to make a memorable drink that will enliven your palate. Depending on the absinthe used, the combination can also turn a stunning verdant color. You will ask yourself: "Oh, has the world changed, or have I changed?"

2 ounces gin

¾ ounce dry vermouth

¾ ounce absinthe

Stir ingredients with ice and strain into a chilled cocktail glass.

Producers: Morrissey, Jonny Marr   Label: Sire

THE CURE

DISINTEGRATION

1989   GENRE: ALTERNATIVE, POST-PUNK, DREAM POP, GOTH   WHEN TO SPIN: DYEING EACH OTHER'S HAIR

A drugged-out tour de force, the Cure's eighth studio album returned to their goth and glam roots to deliver a dream-like classic full of sparkle and revelry. Featuring a few of the band's most beloved songs, such as "Lovesong," "Pictures of You," and "Fascination Street," the record is an introspective and gloomy drone that envelops the listener in a kind of melodic despondency. It works, and it is glorious in its singular mood.

BEFORE YOU DROP THE NEEDLE

Exchange boxes of hair dye, and spread out some newspaper. Or, forget making a mess and just look at old pictures while reminiscing about previous hairstyles.

SIDE A   THE CURE

Created by bartender Gina Chersevani while she was at PS7 in Washington D.C., this is a fine example of a beer-based cocktail. It gets its name from its ability to cure what ails you. Light beer, lemon juice, and ginger? That's a sure stomach settler and hangover helper.

  1 ounce Domaine de Canton ginger liqueur

  5 ounces light lager, such as Miller High Life

  ½ ounce fresh lemon juice

  1 slice fresh ginger, to garnish

Combine ginger liqueur, beer, and lemon juice in a highball glass with ice and stir. Garnish with a slice of ginger on the edge of the glass.

SIDE B   CURE ROYALE

The venerable Kir is made with cassis and white wine (Aligoté, to be precise). A Kir Royale replaces the white wine with Champagne. A Cardinal is Kir with red wine. We like to call a Cardinal with red wine *and* Champagne a Cure Royale. Got all that? Good, now let's get fancy drunk.

  1 ounce crème de cassis

  3 ounces light red wine

  2 ounces Champagne or other sparkling wine

In a wine glass or Champagne flute, combine cassis and wine. Top with Champagne.

OK COMPUTER
RADIOHEAD

LINER NOTES   While their previous album, *The Bends*, might have been their mainstream, guitar-driven break-through, *OK Computer* is where Radiohead pushed their artistry to an experimental new sound—and to international superstardom. The album's layered electronic ambience and intense alienation make for a gripping listen from start to finish. Perhaps not since Pink Floyd's *The Dark Side of the Moon* (page 119), has a band stepped so successfully into the unknown with an album that feels so thoroughly apiece and connected to its audience. It remains a watershed album, a gateway to Radiohead's further abstraction and fragmentation.   **BEFORE YOU DROP THE NEEDLE**   Take off each other's glasses and get comfortable. This is also perfect background music for a Skype date or online connection.

1997 GENRE: ALTERNATIVE ROCK, ELECTRONIC, BRIT-POP
WHEN TO SPIN: NERD BONDING

WHIZZ BANG

This is an album in which human anxiety is mechanized. And this classic cocktail is named after the high velocity shells used during World War I. The shells were dubbed Whizz-Bangs, because all you heard was a whiz and then they exploded. Despite the grim connection, this is a rather serene drink. Essentially a variation on a Rob Roy, the addition of grenadine, orange, and absinthe makes for an inspired libation. Note: two dashes amount to about half a bar spoon.

1½ ounces Scotch

½ ounce sweet vermouth

2 dashes of orange bitters

2 dashes of absinthe

2 dashes of grenadine (page 212)

Stir ingredients with ice and strain into a chilled cocktail glass.

PU-ERH OLD FASHIONED

As quirky as this album is, there's a coziness to it. It's despairing, yet in an introspective way. In this drink, the ur-cocktail (the Old Fashioned, the one from which all others sprang) becomes an alien, resulting in a strange delight. We adapted this drink from food writer Autumn Giles.

Makes 1 cocktail, but enough steeped bourbon for 4

FOR THE PU-ERH-INFUSED BOURBON

1 cup bourbon

2 tablespoons loose leaf pu-erh tea

FOR THE COCKTAIL

2 ounces pu-erh-infused bourbon

4 dashes of Angostura bitters

½ teaspoon sugar

Lemon twist, for garnish

Combine bourbon and tea and let steep for 2 hours. Strain bourbon.

In a rocks glass, muddle sugar and Angostura. Add infused bourbon, ice, and stir. Garnish with a lemon twist.

Producers: Nigel Godrich, Radiohead   Label: Capitol, Parlophone

For Emma, Forever Ago

bon iver

GENRE / indie folk, indie rock **WHEN TO SPIN** / a night by the fire

2007

LINER NOTES

A deeply melancholy album of spare lyrics and dreamy falsetto, Bon Iver's debut album is an ethereal listen. Written while singer-songwriter Justin Vernon spent a winter holed up by himself in a Wisconsin cabin, the record channels illness, life change, and loss (a recent breakup) into a lush soundscape that evokes loneliness and emotional pain with great beauty. Vernon recorded all of the instrumentation himself, intending to create a few demos. He released five hundred copies of the CD at the urging of friends, only to become a sensation after he was discovered and signed by the label Jagjaguwar. The album's eventual mass popularity does not detract from its compelling introspection and intimacy.

BEFORE YOU DROP THE NEEDLE

Keep it simple and let things get contemplative. If you don't have a fireplace, don't sweat it. Just make the place cozy. You can always build a couch fort.

Producer: Justin Vernon   Label: Jagjaguwar

SIDE A LAST WORD

A Prohibition-era drink originally hailing from Detroit, this classic was revived by famed Seattle bartender Murray Stenson at the Zig Zag Café. The cocktail is an herbaceous wonderland, tasting thoroughly modern. The original recipe calls for equal parts gin, Chartreuse, and Maraschino, but good bars these days "ladder" the drink to improve balance. The combination perfectly channels Bon Iver's spectral vibe, and Chartreuse—made by lonely monks in France—fits this album's spare aural landscape.

> 1 ounce gin
> ¾ ounce green Chartreuse
> ½ ounce Maraschino liqueur
> ¾ ounce fresh lime juice
> Lime twist, for garnish

Shake ingredients with ice and strain into a chilled cocktail glass. Garnish with a lime twist.

SIDE B CARIBOU

Never tasted Quebec's cold-weather warmer? Prepare to fall in love with a very compelling drink. Sometimes served out of a cup made of ice, it is the primal taste of the cold North. It's often served during winter outdoor activities, like skiing or at festivals.

> 3 ounces red wine (or Port)
> 1 ounce rye whiskey (or brandy)
> Dash of maple syrup

Combine ingredients in a rocks glass and stir until syrup is well blended. Add ice—preferably one large cube.

BAR CODE

at home

Just as vinyl junkies appreciate sound quality and cover art, the cocktail scene prizes taste and aesthetics. If you need a crash course in bartending, this section will bring you up to speed. Once you move past the red Solo cups, it sure is nice to know how to fix yourself a well-crafted drink. After all, if you're going to spring for good booze, you might as well use fresh ice and a chilled glass. Knowing why these things matter makes all the difference. And—trust us—once you master a few simple bar skills, your paramours will love you even more. Like a first kiss, no one forgets their first real cocktail.

MEASURE THY SPIRITS

A balanced drink makes all the difference. Use a jigger to measure your liquids. Don't try to eyeball it. You know how annoying it is to listen to an LP on the wrong speed? Please, avoid going chipmunks on a good cocktail.

GET FRESH WITH YOUR ICE

Make ice often, and use filtered water. (A Soma or Brita filter works well.) If your water tastes like chlorine, it will throw off the taste of your drink. Also, old ice that tastes like the stale bag of shrimp in the back of your freezer is bad for your social life—who wants a cocktail that smells and tastes vaguely like seafood? Read: ice can absorb off flavors in your freezer, so make a new batch before you invite people over for a party.

Tip: Silicone ice trays are dope—we like the oversize ones that you can use to make big cubes. Bigger cubes melt slowly, which means fewer watery drinks.

USE REAL FRUIT

No self-respecting bartender uses lemon juice from one of those plastic lemons. Or bottled sour mix. But you knew that.

GET YOUR GARNISH GAME ON

A citrus twist isn't purely aesthetic. When you twist a lemon or orange peel over a drink and run it around the rim of the glass (proper technique), you are actually causing a little rainstorm of flavor by releasing oils in the skin onto the surface of the drink. You should be able to *see* the oil floating on your drink after you twisssst.

YOU DON'T NEED FANCY GLASSWARE

But it is nice to chill glasses before serving a cold drink and to warm your mugs before serving hot drinks! To chill a glass, pop it into the freezer for a few minutes. Or keep some coupes in your freezer door. To heat mugs for hot toddies or spiked coffees, fill them with really hot water before you get the drink started.

STIR SPIRITS-ONLY DRINKS

Manhattans and Martinis—they're stirred. You'll hear bartenders refer to them as "spirituous" drinks, because they're made entirely of liquor. Stir them in a mixing glass (after you've filled it $2/3$ of the way up with ice) and spin your bar spoon for about 20 to 30 seconds. Here's the goal: you want your drink to be well chilled and made up of one-quarter ice water.

SHAKE COCKTAILS MADE WITH EGGS, MILK, AND/OR CITRUS

These ingredients need a good shake to help them merge with booze. Fill a shaker a little more than halfway up with ice, then add the remainder of your ingredients. Bartenders like to start with the least expensive ingredient first. Then, cover your shaker—make sure the seal is tight—and shake for 8 to 12 seconds. Then, strain the drink into a prepared glass.

Fear Not the Egg Cocktail

Many early cocktail recipes called for eggs. In fact, there's a whole groups of drinks (flips, nogs, and fizzes) that feature them. Eggs impart a feathery texture and add body. We're required to tell you that people with compromised immune systems may want to veer away from raw eggs in cocktails due to the slight chance of salmonella. So, here are some best practices, along with some easy substitutions:

USING FRESH EGGS

Always gently wash your eggs with soap and water before you use them and make sure they are fresh. We like to use organic eggs, preferably from the local farmers' market. Since eggs vary in size, we measure out ¾ ounce when a drink calls for an egg white.

USING PASTEURIZED EGG WHITES

This is a fine substitute, and many bars use them. You can find cartons of pasteurized egg whites in the cooler section of a grocery. Measure out ¾ ounce when a drink calls for an egg white.

USING POWDERED EGG WHITES

To approximate a single egg white, combine 2 teaspoons of powder, plus 1 ounce of water.

Note: to try a few of our favorite egg cocktails, whip up a Cupid Cocktail (page 81), or a Bosom Caresser (page 183).

Commercial grenadine is sticky sweet and full of red dye (read: we never use it). Originally, the recipe was made from pomegranates, and it was designed to lend exotic tartness to cocktails. We experimented with a variety of homemade combinations until we landed on one we liked. Many versions call for a hit of lemon juice, but we think that a little bit of lime juice instead yields something more sublime. Note: adding an ounce of vodka or bourbon will extend the shelf life of homemade grenadine.

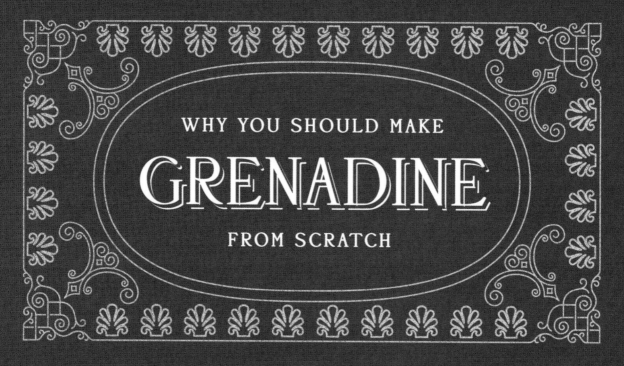

WHY YOU SHOULD MAKE

GRENADINE

FROM SCRATCH

1 cup pomegranate juice (such as POM) ~ 1 cup demerara sugar

2 to 3 drops orange flower water ~ ½ teaspoon fresh lime juice

Pour the pomegranate juice into a small saucepan and add sugar. Stir over medium-low heat until the sugar dissolves, about 3 to 4 minutes. Don't let the mixture boil (it will lose its fresh taste). Remove the pan from the heat and let cool. Then add orange flower water and lime juice. Transfer grenadine to a clean jar, seal well, and refrigerate for up to one month.

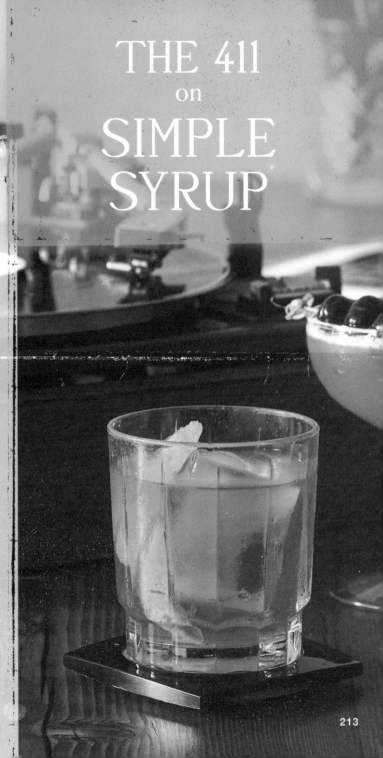

We prefer the taste of demerara sugar to bleached refined sugar. Demerara is a raw sugar, beige in color, and it contains a hint of molasses. The taste really complements dark spirits, like bourbon and rum, but we find that it's delicious in other drinks as well. Know that it does not dissolve quite as easily in water, so you'll need to use heat. If you use refined sugar, you can simply shake equal parts warm water and sugar in a jar and it will dissolve. Note: adding an ounce of vodka to your simple syrup will extend its shelf life.

SIMPLE SYRUP

1 cup demerara sugar

1 cup water

In a small saucepan over medium heat, combine equal parts sugar or water. Stir until the sugar dissolves. Do not boil. Remove the pan from the heat. Cool.

Transfer the liquid to a jar, seal well, and refrigerate for up to a month.

Bar Merch Worth Buying

Let's be real: you can make drinks in a Mason jar and use a chopstick for a stirrer. We've done it. But if you're into having people over for drinks on a semiregular basis, it's handy to have basic bartending tools.

Jigger: The easiest to master for home users is the Oxo jigger. One side measures an ounce. Flip it for an ounce and a half.

Boston Shaker: Two metal cups (or a pint glass and a metal cup) are preferred to the three-piece cobbler shaker. The cups fit snugly together, and you just pop them apart by striking the seal at an angle with the heel of your hand. It takes a little practice, but it's easy if you YouTube a demo.

Bar spoon: A long-handled spoon makes it easy to stir drinks in a mixing glass. Get one with some heft at the handle and you can crack ice with it.

Strainers: There are two kinds of strainers in bartending land: hawthorne and julep. You'll use the hawthorne for shaken drinks—it's the one with a curled spring and stabilizer prongs. When you strain a drink, the spring holds back ice and catches any muddled herbs you might have used. The julep strainer looks like a concave disk with holes, and was originally used to serve mint juleps—it fits over the mixing glass easily and allows for a clean pour.

Citrus press: A handled citrus press is the easiest way to juice loads of lemons or limes for a party. And it holds back most seeds.

Y-peeler: Unless you've got a way with paring knives, the Y-shaped peeler is the easiest way to remove the skin of lemons and oranges when you want to add a twist to a drink. The narrow blade prevents you from grabbing too much of the white pith.

Muddler: When you need to muddle mint or citrus wheels in the bottom of a glass, having a big ol' muddler is handy to express the oils and juices. We started off using a wooden spoon for this, but it doesn't quite have the same effect. Look for a muddler made out of non-reactive wood, like poplar, not something that has varnish that will come off in your drinks.

Glassware: Beware the giant glassware available at many big box stores. For listening parties, your best bet are stemmed cocktail (martini) glasses or coupe glasses—look for ones in the 3½- to 4-ounce range for drinks served "up." For drinks on the rocks, use rocks glasses (also known as lowball or old fashioned) and highball glasses (also known as collins). Scouting estate sales and thrift stores can be a great way to add glassware, just keep an eye on size.

Other useful tools: Cutting board, paring knife, ice bucket, tongs, small sieve, silicone ice trays.

215

Batching Cocktails for a Crowd

Here's a quick way to turn a recipe into eight servings: substitute "cups" for ounces. You can apply this to any recipe. Simply measure the ingredients into a pitcher. Instead of shaking or stirring on ice, dilute the drink by adding 20 percent water. Chill well before serving.

Hold off on batching citrus drinks until right before guests arrive. Citrus juices lose their freshness quickly, especially when mixed with spirits, so to keep a pitcher of Margaritas zesty, batch out the spirits ahead of time. Then squeeze your citrus right before guests arrive.

INDEX

ACKNOWLEDGMENTS

It's been an honor and a privilege to write this, our third book together, in just under four years. We never imagined when we started shaking and stirring together during our online hangouts that we would be given the opportunity (nay, the incentive!) to keep drinking—professionally. Thank you, Running Press, for jumping on our proposals, spurring us on, and turning our ideas into such stunning books. Huge thanks to editor Cindy De La Hoz, designer Josh McDonnell, and publicist Seta Zink. Thank you, Amy Williams, for keeping your eye on the needle; thank you, Jason Varney and Kristi Hunter, for making music for the eyes.

If this project were a record, we would dedicate songs to the following people who have saved, supported, and inspired us: Sonja Darlington, Mahlon Darlington, Alice Pfister, Todd Stregiel, Marisa Dobson, Mike Landers, Tina Breslow, Oleg Lyubner, Frederick Hanson (DJ Foundation), DJ Mike Carlson, DJ Nick Nice, Michael Horowitz (DJ Fuzzy Duck), Jess Conaway, Freedy Johnston, Duke Erickson, Ken Fitzsimmons, Paul Creswell, Tom Baker, Joe and Connie Davis, Elizabeth Davis, Wade Harrison, Michele Tjader, Penn Jensen, Monique Huston, Michael Reynolds, Gerald Rose, Tom Cranley, Ken Backus, Brian Haltinner, Robert Whitlock, Caitlin Kolberg, David Hammond, Tom Loup, Kristi Genna, Natasha Nicholson, Ben Granby, James "Pi" Cowan, Tristan Gallagher, Jay Moran, Emily Ellis, Jeff Burke, F. Stokes, Jeff and Jacqui Jahnke, Addie Juell, Shannon Berry, Jen Edmonds, Grant Hurless, Genevieve Visse, Maeraj Sheikh, Melodie DeWitt, Apollo Marquez, Cris Comello, Tom Miller, John Skyler, Susan and Jonathan Lipp, Ron Laxamana, Ellen Yin and everyone at High Street Hospitality, Jonny Medlinsky and the super staff at Martha, the gang at The Keep, Sue Miller, Mike Geno, Matt Buddah, Wendy Schneider, Alexis Siemons, Marisa McClellan, Amanda Feifer, Joy Manning, Stef Patrizio, Aimee Knight, Phil Charron and everyone at Think Company, the staff at *Isthmus*, the Di Bruno Bros. crew, the English Department of Saint Joseph's University, the staff at Philadelphia's Lokal Hotel, and spontaneous hand models Tyler Widdick and Mike Massucci.

ANDRÉ
AND
TENAYA